UNLOCKING THE SECRET OF OTHERLAND

A story and activity book for children living abroad

Mieke M.E. Janssen-Matthes
Illustrations Frans Kwakkenbos
KIT Publishers – Amsterdam

Unlocking the Secret of Otherland. A story and activity book for children living abroad.
Mieke M. E. Janssen-Matthes. Illustrations Frans Kwakkenbos.

Original title: *Het geheim van Anderland. Een lees- en doeboek voor kinderen die in het buitenland wonen.*
Mieke M.E. Janssen-Matthes. Illustraties Frans Kwakkenbos. Amsterdam 2006.

KIT Publishers
Mauritskade 63
Postbus 95001
1090 HA Amsterdam
E-mail: publishers@kit.nl
Website: www.kit.nl/publishers

Illustrations: Frans Kwakkenbos, Schalkhaar, the Netherlands
Editor: Nancy Forest-Flier, Alkmaar, the Netherlands
Lay out: Frans Kwakkenbos, Schalkhaar, the Netherlands
Production: Meester & De Jonge, Lochem, the Netherlands

ISBN 90 6832 587 6

NUR 200 / 228

About the author
Educational psychologist and interculturalist Mieke M.E. Janssen-Matthes has more than twenty years experience counseling, consulting, and teaching children and adults living international and intercultural lives.

Books on Intercultural communication available at KIT Publishers (in English):
Dealing with the Dutch, J. Vossestein
Living with the Dutch, Norean Radke Sharpe
Dealing with Differences, N. Vink

For my grandchildren who inspire me.
For Rabirius, my anchor.

Contents

Preface for parents and teachers

This book is written as an activity book for children who will be living abroad for an extended period of time. The basic idea is to guide the child in thought, imagination and activity – in reading, writing and doing – and to explore and try to understand the many confusing situations that can occur in a new country. He'll meet children in stories who are going through similar experiences, see parallels in the various examples and be stimulated to look at the world from a different perspective. In this way cultural differences and similarities are addressed and discussed. Problems are not hidden but clarified.

This book will show children how they can come to grips with difficulties rising from a new, culturally different situation. It will describe the frustrations and surprises that might come their way – but without forgetting the fun and magic of a new life! By keeping a diary the reader will learn to look at himself and to consider the changes of his life in Otherland.
For parents and children alike, embarking on a long stay abroad as a family, or within a new family, can be exhausting. A lot of things need to be taken care of, all at the same time. A new job, a new place to live, a new school – all these require your attention. Added to this are the different surroundings, including changes in climate, language and culture. At the same time you'll miss the circle of friends and family you've always been able to rely on. At times you may feel as if you've been hit by a tidal wave that has swept you onto an unknown shore! Finding a new rhythm will demand care and attention.
As you experience this you'll see that the changes are even greater for children, because leaving home wasn't their idea. They might be lacking in motivation. They're also sensitive to the stressful family situation caused by change and re-orientation. They could perceive this as threatening – just when they're in urgent need of a sense of guaranteed safety. This is when children require extra attention and care, when parents are preoccupied with so many other things in order to get the family settled.
Unlocking the Secret of Otherland has been developed to support young people in this period of change and settling in. Working in a book like this will help make it easier for a child to get his bearings in new surroundings. It will offer him support in grappling with or getting around obstacles in a process of growth and personal development. Feelings linked with culture shock are treated in such a way that children can understand the underlying process.

Using this book will not cause difficulties to melt away, but it might form a firm basis for building a happy life in your new situation.

Wishing you a happy life in Otherland!

Mieke M.E. Janssen-Matthes, educational psychologist

* When I refer to parents in the following text I also include educators, teachers and caretakers.
I have alternately used 'he' or 'she' in reference to young persons.

Preface for readers and go-getters

This is a book made especially for you. It was written for you and for all other children who have moved away from their home country to a new land. It could be any country in the world, and it would be impossible to name them all. That's why I've called it 'Otherland'.
But you can use the real name of your new country instead. You can fill that name in here:
.... is my Otherland.

It's true that this book was made especially for you, because you're one of the many young people who have moved from one country to another. You are among the young nomads who are learning how adventurous and difficult it can be to live in a different country. Just leaving your homeland is tough. It's not easy for those kids, and it's not easy for you either.
You'll encounter a lot of new things: a different school, a different home, people talking a strange language. And that's just the beginning! That's what this book is about – all those changes. About the funny things and the not-so-funny things. About how you can turn the new and different things into a game, and really have fun. You'll discover *the Secret of Otherland.*
So, off you go.

Before you start reading this very special book, I must tell you something. This book, *Unlocking the Secret of Otherland,* is an activity book and a reading book at the same time. That means that you can sit back, relax and read. But that's only part of it. In between the stories you'll find questions to answer and little tasks to do. What are these all about? Do this, do that, imagine this, make that – all sorts of ways to be as creative as you like. You'll see for yourself when you start. This is the activity part. You can write down the results of your work in the book as well. As you write, you'll turn the book into a book of your own. There won't be any other book like it in the whole world. And when you're done you'll have lots of reasons to be very proud. Working in this book is like eating plums. Finishing the book in a big rush may be more than you can stomach. It isn't meant to be done that way. A few pages a day is a good pace. That way you'll keep on liking it and you'll finish it, too. Just like the bowl of plums. 'A page a day keeps the pain away'.

To help you pace yourself I've made an activities calendar, or act prop. You'll see this calendar on the next page. Every week you finish one chapter. When the weekend comes you'll have a chance to write in your diary if your week was too busy. If you find a chapter is difficult, take more time and then ask for help. Keep on going. Other chapters will be easier or more fun. Every time you finish a task, circle it on your calendar as 'done'. By going at this speed you can finish your book in three months. And believe me, that's really fast for making your own book. Not only that, but you'll know *the Secret of Otherland* as well. And that's fantastic.

Now, get going. Be sure to ask for help if you need it. Enjoy yourself, and have fun!

CALENDAR OF ACTIVITIES - ACT PROP

TO DO		DONE
1.	Living in an other land	○
2.	Inside and outside	○
3.	Me and my others	○
4.	Do-it-yourself	○
5.	School	○
6.	In the classroom	○
7.	Friends, family and festivities	○
8.	Difficult moments	○
9.	Homesick	○
10.	We and they	○
	Unlocking the secret	○

All done? Well done!
Congratulations, you unlocked the secret!

Chapter 1

Living in an other land

THE BEGINNING

In your home country you must have read and heard about your Otherland. But now it's reality and you're living there. You find that it's different from what you thought it would be like. That's usually the way it is. You're sure there are many surprises in store for you. You can use this book as you think about these unexpected happenings. You'll soon find that it can help you deal with what you don't understand, and with the things that are happening in your daily life. You can write about it, make drawings, take pictures, read more and talk to others.

In this way you'll build your own story, and by making your own story you'll become more comfortable in your new setting. This book will teach you how to grow new roots. People are like plants in some ways. A plant from your neighbor's garden will grow in your garden if you care for it: give it a pleasant place, water and fertiliser. The important thing is to take care of yourself. You've been transplanted to fresh soil, roots and all. This book could be the water and the fertiliser!

NOW IT'S YOUR TURN

I began writing and you did the reading. Now it's your turn to write. Start by writing about the main character in your book: you, of course! Then tell a little about what has happened so far.

This is how your story starts. Step by step you'll write an adventure story or a kind of diary about your life in Otherland. In this story, all the different pieces will come together to form the secret of Otherland. All the new people around you, the different language and the strange food – not to mention all the other things – seem totally unconnected at first. Only when you have a good look at them, when you observe them for quite some time, do they become like pieces of a jigsaw puzzle: they'll all fit together and make a beautiful new picture, a happy new life. So I'll take you by the hand. Go ahead and start your book.

MY BOOK
It will be called:
THE SECRET OF OTHERLAND

My name is: ....

Now I live in: ....

My new address is: ....

....

....

My part of the world is called: ....

I used to live in: ....

....

....

We came to Otherland because: ....

....

....

This may not be easy for you. There's nothing wrong with that. It's hard to write about difficult things. Try the best you can or just ask your family and talk about it. You'll feel better when you understand why something happened.

MY SURROUNDINGS

When you look around you it's obvious that you live in a different country. You notice it everywhere. Even the address you just wrote down is written in a different way. Addresses sometimes clearly show the differences between countries. Look again at your own two addresses, the old one and the new one. Are the house numbers placed in the same spot? Are the houses numbered or named? And what about the streets? Or is this an address that describes the location: 200 meters north of the Cathedral, then 800 meters due west, the white house on your left-hand side? A bit different from 23 River Tower, 3 SE 26th Rd? You see what I mean? Sometimes there are only postbox addresses, which are very practical for collecting your mail when you live far out in the country, where there are no addresses or the addresses are too complicated.

So you see how something as simple as an address can tell you a lot. Anyhow, it tells you that you're living in Otherland.

More things tell you that you're in Otherland. Look closely around once again. Look at your house, the time, the weather, the people, the sounds or the noise and the smells, to mention a few things – things that are different here in Otherland.

What makes you know you're in Otherland?

MY SURROUNDINGS ARE DIFFERENT HERE IN OTHERLAND

I know this

because: ....

because: ....

because: ....

and ....

....

....

This takes some getting used to! If only your old friends back home could see you now! Have you sent them a postcard yet? Don't forget. It'll make them happy.

A STORY – LIKE ALICE

You've been in Otherland for quite a while now. It took some time before you could start your book. Your jetlag is over, but maybe you still need a bit more sleep. Go ahead. All these new impressions make you tired, too.

Maybe you feel a bit like 'Alice in Wonderland'. Alice, a young teenager, goes on an eerie dream-journey and arrives in a magic world she can hardly understand. In her misery she cries a pool of tears she can swim in. Sometimes she grows so fast that her hair gets tangled in the branches of trees. Other times she shrinks and shrinks till she's smaller than a toadstool! But to her the hardest thing is that she cannot understand the way people behave and communicate in this magic world. It is all so strange!

'Why is everything so different?' she keeps asking herself. 'I don't like feeling so stupid!' she says with a sigh. Not understanding her world sometimes makes her sad. And it should. In the story this happens to Alice, but in reality it could happen to you.

By now you'll understand these feelings. They're all part of what it's like to spend a long time abroad. Alice often doesn't know how to react. Should she cry, laugh or get angry? The smartest thing she does, however, is to observe her world. Because she doesn't understand, she keeps looking at the magic and asking questions. She keeps asking and doesn't make judgments – is it good? is it bad? – because she just wants to know why things happen the way they do. And you, can you make them 'unhappen'? *Observing carefully and not deciding right away whether something is right or wrong* is what helped Alice in Wonderland. Does it work for you, too?

SOME GOOD ADVICE

Now read the next lines out loud until you nearly know them by heart. You're going to need them, again and again...

Not knowing
what to do,
or where to turn?
Stop and look,
listen and learn.

Not knowing
what to do,
where's the link?
Stop and look,
listen and think.

Still don't know?
What a difficult task!
Stop and look,
listen and ask.

It worked for Alice in Wonderland. How happy she was to find that everyone was willing to help. Those were the good things for Alice in her Wonderland. That way she made new friends, too, friends who taught her magic.

LAUGHING AND CRYING

How are you doing? To Alice it was just a special dream. She wakes up at the end of the story on a bench in her own garden where she fell asleep in the sunshine. But you live for real in your Otherland. When you wake up you're still living in this new place. You'll have to solve your riddles your own way. With the help of your book.

You just saw some drawings of a child. Look at them well. Then pick and choose the ones you like. Do you notice the different expressions? It's like Alice in the story.

Now you draw some different expressions in the blank faces in the next illustration. As you do this, imagine the feelings you have when your face looks like this. Think about the situations you're in that give you these feelings sometimes.

HOW DO I FEEL?

Now that you're familiar with these faces and expressions you can use them in the following text. Of course you can add some words as well.

In my new home I feel drawing

At school I like to look

The weather here is mostly

I'd love to be friends with

IS IT HARD TO MAKE YOUR OWN STORY?

You may still be thinking: How on earth do I make my own book? But see what you've done? You've already started! Believe me, the rest will be just as easy as this. In the open spaces write what's important to you.

Draw whatever you like best, whatever you don't understand, or whatever you think is different.

You could also make lists of what's happening around you: 'First this happened, then this, then this...'

Think about things in your own way. That's how you make your book special.

I'll give you some examples of how children wrote about their experiences in their Otherland. It's as easy as that. Their stories may help you become more observant.

EXAMPLES

* A Dutch boy, 11 years old, describes his arrival in China:
'Today we arrived in China. The bus is going through the streets of Peking. The streets are packed with bicyclists, ringing their bells long and loud. Cars are continuously hooting their horns. Girls walk hand in hand. Men are walking arm in arm. Everywhere you see tea houses, and rows of small wooden shops. Men are crouched, sitting in the streets, spitting out sunflower pits. Women are washing clothes in small basins in front of their small houses in the streets. People, people, people wherever you look. Eyes and more eyes staring at us. A man on a bicycle hit a tree because he kept staring at us way back there…'

* Another boy, age 9, writes: 'I live in Shanghai garden. I always play with my friend. I'm telling you now about Shanghai: too many high buildings, too many streets, lots of time in traffic jams and far too many people. Too many hotels. They always spit and eat with chop sticks, they're always pushing.'

* A girl, age 10, writes down what she sees when she goes to the market in her Otherland. 'Today I see: * a wash line with live pigeons on it, * a vendor helping 5 clients at the same time, * heaps of mangos at 12 cents a piece, * dead birds for eating.'

Now it's your turn. Do your best. Why not write about what you see in your new life? First say to yourself, *'stop and look, listen and learn, listen and think'*.
If you've got a camera – or you can borrow one – take some pictures of the world around you, the things you think are special, strange or funny, and maybe important. But take care. In some countries you're not allowed to photograph buildings or people. When in doubt, ask first. Always *'stop, look, listen and ask'* before you take pictures – I do that myself. You can paste the pictures in your book as well.

Make it part of your own story. This is how you write about your daily life, the life you now live in Otherland. By looking at it this way you'll understand it sooner and much better. So, stop and write! You'll be much happier!

WHAT I DID AND SAW TODAY

....

....

....

....

....

....

....

....

....

Now you've come to the end of chapter 1. Here's a short list of the contents of this chapter, to make it easy when you're browsing later on.

A SHORT LIST

In this chapter you started collecting pieces of your secret of Otherland. So far you know that:

* life in Otherland is really different from the life you used to live,
* there's a lot in Otherland you don't understand,
* living in a new country requires lots of observation,
* you learn by asking when you don't understand,
* a little poem is a good reminder,
* it's normal to feel sad and tired sometimes,
* writing a diary is a great way to feel better,
* you don't judge, but learn to understand.

In the next chapter we'll discover more pieces of your secret. But before you start, here's some open space for writing down the things you'd like to remember later on. Or for any extra things you want to jot down.

MY DIARY

Chapter 2

Inside and outside

In this chapter you'll get to know more about yourself and others, and about staying at home and going in search of adventures. About inside and outside. You've already written in your book that so many things are different here compared with your homeland. But you'll also notice that lots of things are the same. Just read on.

WHO AM I?

In the first chapter you wrote down your name and address. You wrote about how you like your surroundings. You drew faces to show your feelings. Now you can show who you really are. You – the 'main character' in this book.
Do you have a picture of yourself? If you do, paste it in the middle of the following illustration. A nice drawing of yourself will do just fine if you don't have a picture.
All around this picture make a circle of drawings or pictures of:

* your family,
* the food you like best,
* your favorite pastime,
* your favorite color,
* your favorite animal,
* your best friend,
* the nicest TV program.

If you find there's something missing from this list, go ahead and add it.

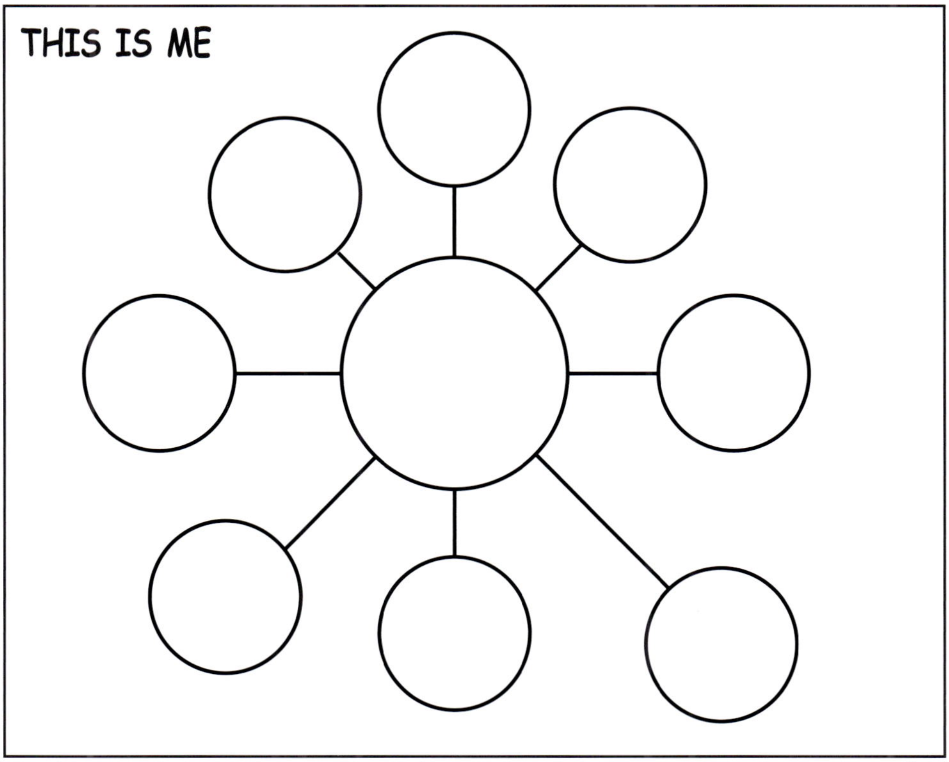

You could also turn this into a little rhyme:

I am who I am,
said the fox.
I am who I am,
said the hare.
We are aware
no one's the boss!

I'm tall, you're small
said the fox to the hare,
be aware.
No one could call
us the same!

Yes, all of us are different.
To me it is just excellent,
forever and always to be,
just me!

You could also make a mobile. Here's how.
You only need a coat hanger (even a stick will do), some leftover packaging material and a pair of scissors. Paste your pictures on pieces of cardboard. Punch holes at the top of each piece. Thread the pieces and connect them to the coat hanger.
Put yourself at the top! There you are – all ready.

MY HOME

Once your mobile is finished you might hang it near your bed. This way you can see all the people who are important to you – the people who belong to you and who care for you. It's very nice to have your family around when you're in a new country, where everything is new and unfamiliar. You're special then, because when you're at home with your family you can understand each other. At home you can share what you've experienced in the outside world. At home you might also show what you're writing and doing in your new book. And at home there's always someone to help when you're stuck with one of your activities. Don't forget: *Stop and look, listen and ask!* You might think of lots more nice things about being with your family at home. Try to list them:

MY HOME

At home I like to

....

And to ....

....

I do this alone or together with ....

....

But what I like best is ....

....

Remember: your family is important, whether they're nearby or far away. Keep in touch. Home is part of you. It belongs to you and your family. You might even enjoy being together more now that you're in Otherland. Because you're still new in Otherland, I hope you'll soon have a pleasant place or a cozy corner in your new home to call your own, a place where you can play or work in your book. Later on your family's larger pieces of baggage will arrive if they were shipped separately. This sometimes happens if you've moved far away. How nice it will be to rediscover the old familiar things.

OTHERLAND

At home you speak your own language, but beyond your home and garden is Otherland. That's the outside world. There you'll find familiar things as well as mysterious things. Outside they speak Otherlandish, they communicate in the Otherland way.
In the beginning that's very hard to deal with. Try to learn it as quickly as possible. You cannot learn it soon enough. At home they'll find opportunities to start learning the language. You can do the hard work there. One of the secrets of Otherland, however, is that you learn most of the language by playing with other children, by making friends. Just join them and see what happens. Now look at the illustration and fill in the empty clouds with your reasons for learning Otherlandish.

In case you'd like to see my reasons turn to the end of this chapter.

THE SHREWD FOX

Before you know it you'll be a shrewd fox yourself. You're doing very well.
You can either be a shrewd and brainy fox or a shy hare.
But in Otherland you don't have to be shy or afraid. Discover your new world. There's so much to see, so many different things, so many other people. Remind yourself: *look, stop and try to understand. And when you don't understand: just ask!*
It doesn't help to be shy.

But fortunately not everything is different. Have a look around you.

ALL OVER THE WORLD

All over the world people have the same wish: to live a happy life. With this in mind they make the most of their situation: they look for the best solutions. Notice how they build their houses, from high-rise buildings to shacks made of cardboard boxes. How they dress in different kinds of clothes or eat different kinds of food. They do this for good reasons – reasons we don't always know about. It's their best solution. All over the world people have their own ways of living their lives. Rich people, poor people. In your country they did it your way. You liked it. But keep in mind that it's just one way of doing things, one solution that works in that country.

Outside your door in Otherland you can see and learn a great deal – and have a lot of fun besides! There's so much that you've never seen before. That's one of the nice things about living abroad.

Be curious and be a shrewd fox. Forget the shy hare.

A PENNY FOR YOUR THOUGHTS?

Now that you're feasting your eyes in Otherland, what do you think? What do you like about it all?
You thought about this before you came, of course, but now that you're here – what's it like for you? Is it nice, irritating or what? Just make a note of your first impressions. Add the date – it'll be useful later on!

MY FIRST IMPRESSIONS

Date:
This is what I now:

like	don't like
....	....
....	....
....	....
....	....
....	....

Why don't you ask your family what their impressions are?

My family now

likes	doesn't like
....	....
....	....
....	....

You and your family together might find solutions for the irritating things. Take the dangerous dog you have to pass on your way to school. You feel braver if you walk past him with your sister! Or maybe you're the only one with this particular problem. Look at it in another way: make friends with the dog and the problem is solved.

Sometimes the problem can't be solved and you'll have to learn to live with it – too many people, or too much dust, or too much traffic. Sometimes the things you like may be irritating to your brother. Making lots of new girlfriends in the neighborhood, for instance, while there are no boys his age around.

You could even turn these likes and dislikes into a game.

A NEW GAME

You could make a set of cards and write your likes and dislikes on them, one on each card. Leave the other side blank. Each person playing the game takes 3 cards.
You explain the rules. Make a pile of the cards. Then everyone in turn takes a card and reads it out loud and together you talk about it. You ask the first question: 'Why would anyone like or dislike this?' Have a good guess. The next question is 'Who wrote this down?' Then this person tells why he wrote this down.
If it was a 'dislike' card, you ask 'What can we do about it, how can we help?'
If it was a 'like' card, the question is 'What can we do to keep it like that?'
Maybe there's nothing you can do about some dislikes, like the weather. You can always start brainstorming. The player with the best answers may now ask the questions and turn the cards.

This may soon turn into a game you play with your friends or family, say once a month for a certain period of time. It's a kind of 'Don't worry' game. As the months pass, you'll see that some old 'dislike' cards aren't necessary anymore. In fact, what you disliked at first you might even end up liking. Move them to the other pile, or paste them in your scrapbook if you don't feel strongly about them any more. Or start a new round of cards.

This is what the next chapter is all about: how to make the pile of 'like' cards higher. How to make the most of your stay in Otherland.

Now you've come to the end of chapter 2. Here's a short list of the contents, to make it easy when you're browsing later on.

A SHORT LIST

Now that you've finished two chapters you know that in Otherland you

* are making your own book,
* will create a nice new home,
* will talk things over with your family and friends,
* must learn the new language,
* will learn most of all from your native friends,
* should be curious, not shy,
* still do not understand everything, but *stop and look, listen and learn.*

But before you start with the next chapter, here's some open space for writing down the things you'd like to remember later on. Or for any extra things you want to jot down. (My answers to the questions on page 17 would be: I'd like to talk to my friends; be happy in class, read Otherlandish books and watch and understand TV).

MY DIARY

Chapter 3

Me and my others

In chapter 2 you learned how to take a better look at yourself, your family and your surroundings. Now you know more about them. It's time to move on and start reading chapter 3.

WHO'S DIFFERENT?

When you still lived in your home country you were just one kid out of many – pretty ordinary, I suppose. As long as you didn't have an outstanding feature that drew people's attention, you were OK. You had no idea what being different really meant. You didn't know how it felt.

Maybe you saw it happening around you: new kids in school or in your neighborhood. They may have moved from a different part of the country or from abroad.
They were different, not like you. You belonged to the group who knew the unspoken rules and regulations. In fact, you probably took those rules for granted. But the newcomers had no idea. They felt strange and uncomfortable.

In school and at home you were probably taught that people are equal, they're basically all the same, all human beings, and you have to respect others, to be nice. But still, playing with kids you know – who understand your language, who know the rules – is more fun. And it's just easier. The others might join in, of course, but they had to play according to the rules of your group.
You belonged to the in-group, 'us'. The others were the out-group, 'them'.
Do you remember this happening?

THE TOPSY-TURVY WORLD

And now in Otherland it's happening to you. Now it is your turn, the topsy-turvy world. You're the conspicuous one. You're the newcomer. You belong to the out-group, 'them', instead of the in-group, 'us'. This requires some major adjustments. It isn't easy. How come? Let me tell you.

Why do you think the Otherland children think you're different? In order to answer this question you have to start looking at the Otherland children, just the way you learned to do this in the previous chapter. Look at them when you're shopping, cycling or sitting in your car, on a park bench or just walking around where kids are playing. *Stop and look. Observe.* – If you're already in school, observing is very easy and you certainly notice a lot. There will be more in the next chapter. –

At home you write your observations down in your book. Have you noticed any differences? Try to write down what you saw:

KIDS IN OTHERLAND - ARE THEY DIFFERENT FROM ME?

I find that they:

....

....

....

....

....

Here the secret is this: that what you see as differences in others, the others see as differences in you. Topsy-turvy! A change of perspective. You see something from a different point of view.

This isn't simple at all, even to grown-ups! So I'll give you some examples.

SOME EXAMPLES

If you stand in the middle of the staircase and you look at your sister at the top of the stairs, she'll say that you're down – standing lower than she is. She's up, you're down – according to her perception. But your little brother, at the foot of the stairs, sees you as up, high on the stairs. That's his perception. As a result you're being seen as high and low at the same time, or as up and down at the same time. Confusing? Then try it and see for yourself.

If you find that people in Otherland are loud when they talk together, they'll think for sure that you are so soft-spoken. So people from your country speak normally and softly at the same time.

In France, an American is seen as a foreigner. In the US, however, a Frenchman is seen as the strange European, the foreigner. So a kid can be native French, European and foreign at the same time depending on the perspective.

The first example is a good one to try out. You did it already? You can also have a try with 'first and last', 'in front of and behind'. Walk around two objects and your perspective changes!

Or you stay in one place while someone else walks around you. According to them, you could be in front and then behind – even though you didn't move your feet! Look at the example again if you still need some extra help.

CHANGING POINTS OF VIEW

It's exactly this change in viewpoints that makes life in Otherland difficult. You know this now. But experiencing it in your daily life is different and sometimes very confusing. To go back to the example: you think you're high up, they think you're way down low! So *stop and look, listen and learn* and *stop and think*.

Think how you might change your own perspective. To use the example: by stepping aside or climbing the stairs to turn 'in front of' into 'behind' and 'up' into 'down'.

Do you remember the first chapter? *Stop and look, listen and learn, stop and ask.* Do you remember how Alice looked at her Wonderland? Not by judging, but by looking and asking – and asking again. Because the more you know, the more you understand. That's helpful now in discovering points of view.

You just wrote down how you see Otherland children differ from you.

Now change your point of view. Get a different perspective.
This calls for imagination – you have it, you can do it. You're young.
Try to write it down as well:

KIDS IN OTHERLAND, DO THEY THINK I'M DIFFERENT?

I think they see me as:

* ....
* ....
* ....
* ....

You see? You can do it. It's very natural, because most things have more than one side. The dollar has a front and a back, and so do you! There's a top and a bottom, a left and a right side. And when you quarrel with your sister, your mother wants to hear your sister's story as well. The other perspective!

DIFFERENT BUT ALSO THE SAME

In observing the differences you also noticed the similarities – because you looked so carefully, of course. Not everything is the same, isn't it? You read this in the other chapters. And you know that many things are the same as well. Just think: all children like to be loved. All children love to eat well, to have a warm and dry place to sleep, clean air and space to breathe and play in. They want just what you want. Is there more you can think of that is the same for all people, no matter where they live? Add it to your book in the next paragraph.

KIDS IN OTHERLAND ARE JUST LIKE ME

* They love their parents
* They don't like to be hungry
* ....
* ....
* ....
* ....

If you haven't been living in Otherland very long, the best you can do is to pay more attention to the similarities than to the differences. Don't worry about the 'otherness'. Deep down inside, you know that all kids are the same. They like to play, to learn and to be happy. Try to join. Later on, the differences – the real differences inside, the ones you don't notice at first – become more important. By then you will have been living longer in this country and speaking the language. We'll leave that for later.

NORMAL?

You've read and thought about what's different and what's the same. 'Normal' is another category that fits in here. How often have you heard people say, 'That's not normal'? How often have you heard people talk about 'normal behavior'?

But what is normal? Normal has a double meaning, too. Normal, says the dictionary, 'is regular, typical or conforming to a standard'. And what is not regular or not conforming to the standard is abnormal, different. Every child being raised in his or her home country wants to behave according to the standards of that country. He wants to be loved and praised, he wants to be like the others – just normal. As you were in your country.

Now you can see that children in a different country live according to a different standard. All societies – people living together – form their own standard, their own norms. It is very likely that what is normal here is not your understanding of normal. This is sometimes very confusing, especially when you've been living in Otherland for some time. It's also an important piece of the secret of Otherland.

It's your challenge to learn to live with different standards, different 'normals'. There is a norm for inside, and one for outside. Sometimes you have to live at home and in school according to different rules and regulations. What you're allowed to do at home, you cannot do at school. Good behavior in school or with friends is bad behavior at home. This is something you can learn! Do you have examples? Here's some open space to use for your example.

WHERE NORMAL IS NOT NORMAL

My example:

At home I'm allowed to: ....

At school I'm not allowed to do this.

At school I'm supposed to: ....

At home this doesn't happen.

Here are more examples of different standards. Maybe you recognize some of them.

NORMS ARE DIFFERENT. IT SHOWS!

In some countries children have a set bedtime. All the children in your group went to bed at roughly the same time, which you always thought was too early (and of course you thought your friends always went to bed later!). Maybe you now live in a country where even babies go to bed really late. That's normal here. As a result your normal bedtime will change, too, and you'll be going to bed much later as well. Aren't you lucky?

Maybe in Otherland you're not allowed to wear shoes when you enter the classroom, and that includes you. At home you don't have to take off your shoes at the front door.

Kids in the neighborhood come and play at your house. They're curious and they love to play with your stuff. You don't always like it – but come on, in this country there aren't many Legos or electric toys. So you share and let them play as well. Then you notice things vanishing every now and then. You stop hesitating and you tell your parents about your suspicion. The parents talk with the kids, and it seems that for them this is normal among friends. To you it's not.

In this country boys play with boys and girls play with girls. This may happen in your family, too. But in some countries girls are strictly forbidden to play with boys. Even so, the boys have a mean way of bullying the girls, who are afraid to complain. To them this is normal. You think this is not normal at all.

You should always talk to your parents about difficult situations. Now you know how important your home – your background – is for you in Otherland. This has to do with 'different' and 'normal' too. The people at home also recognize the differences. There you can talk about what puzzles or worries you. Don't worry on your own. Remember the little poem? Exactly.

Stop and look
Listen and learn,
Talk about it
One more time

Now do you understand that in Otherland you have to be different as well? You have to behave differently with outsiders. You have to adapt to Otherland rules if you want to join in the games. The change of perspective will help you a lot.

There's an old saying: 'When in Rome, do as the Romans do'. That means acting like everybody around you, because what they do is normal. That's how you learned things when you were very young: by imitating. But only imitate 'the right Romans'. This works fine until you get into situations like those described in two of the examples above.

When you think: this is really not normal, or: I don't want to do this, then ask someone what to do.
Don't do anything you think is wrong.

MORE SUPPORT

In the other chapters you learned how to manage in Otherland on your own, adapting your behavior to the situation. In this chapter you'll read stories about how to deal with other problems. Adventures make you inventive!

Life is more complex now – and more interesting, too. It's a nuisance when you don't speak the language fluently, but this will improve day by day. Don't despair! There's lots of support out there to help you settle down in your new home.

Here's part of a story you may remember, *Puss-in-Boots*. See what it can do for you.

LIKE *PUSS-IN-BOOTS*

This is a story about poor Hans, the youngest son of a miller. When his father died, all Hans inherited was a cat. But this was a very shrewd cat – and very inventive as well. And on top of everything else, the cat could talk! All this didn't make Hans into a rich man, though. Actually Hans was very poor. Then one day the cat heard the king's carriage coming, and he said to his master, 'Take off your clothes and jump into the river, quick!' Hans immediately jumped into the river and the cat hid his clothing in the bushes. As the king's carriage was passing the cat started shouting and crying, 'Stop, please stop! Help, oh help! My master the Marquis of Carrabas is drowning!' The carriage came to a halt and the king's servants fetched Hans from the water. The king gave the dripping Hans his own coat and took him into his carriage. Then they looked for his clothes. Where were they? Stolen, they thought. The cat was silent. In the carriage there was a beautiful princess, the king's daughter. She immediately fell head over heels in love with Hans while riding to the king's castle. There Hans was given beautiful clothes. Now he looked just like a real Marquis of Carrabas.

Of course the king and the princess, who was so much in love, wanted to take Hans back to his own home. They longed to see how he lived, how beautiful the palace of Carrabas was.

Hans was at his wit's end. He had no idea how to solve this problem. He had no home, let alone a palace. And they were being so nice to him, the princess was so sweet! But the cat was sure to find a way out. 'I shall go back to the palace first and have them prepare everything for your arrival,' he said to Hans, the king and the princess.

The cat left. Along the way he told the people he met that if the king asked whose land this was, tell him it was owned by the Marquis of Carrabas. Don't forget, he said.

And sure enough, on his way the king was impressed by all the land owned by the Marquis. 'Everything I see is yours, the people tell me. How rich you must be,' said the king to Hans in the carriage. Hans didn't say much. He sat there filled with shame.

In the meantime the cat arrived at a castle where a giant lived. This giant was a witch as well. The cat persuaded the giant to turn himself into a lion. 'Absolutely fabulous,' said the cat, 'but I bet you couldn't shrink down and turn into a mouse.' 'Of course I could,' said the lion-giant. 'Just look at me now.' And he turned himself into a little mouse. 'Got you,' said the cat, who pounced on him and ate him up. The giant was no more.

In the distance the cat heard the king's carriage approaching. He made a deep bow and invited them into the castle. There a delicious dinner was ready, prepared for the giant in his wonderful palace.

The king was so impressed by all this that he wanted his daughter, the princess, to marry the Marquis. By this time Hans was very much in love, too, and he instantly consented. Now he was so rich that his cat didn't have to catch another mouse as long as he lived! Hans and his princess – and the cat – lived happily ever after.

OLD WISDOM

Old wisdom about life is often hidden in old fairy tales. It's hidden here, too. In this story, Hans had no idea what was going to happen next, or how to solve his desperate situation. He only knew that he was very worried, at his wit's end. By listening carefully to the advice of someone he hardly believed at all, everything turned out OK – even though the cat's normal behavior wasn't at all what he would consider normal!

It shows us that no matter how difficult the situation might be, solutions can always be found with a little imagination and creative thinking – and by trusting someone creative who thinks differently.

So when you find yourself in difficult situations, be inventive like Puss-in-Boots and trust your friend, as Hans did. It could come in handy.

A FRIEND

You saw in the story that having your own Puss-in-Boots can be a great support. Look for a loyal friend to help you, a person in Otherland who knows her way around, knows the ins and outs of Otherland. A person who can explain what you don't understand.

Find a friend in Otherland, someone you like and trust. It could be a young friend, a neighbor, someone who works in your house or garden or a friend of the family. Or maybe it's the parents of a new friend. *Look and listen, observe and you'll find.* Some kids go to a librarian they like and trust for support. Others prefer a teacher or counselor.

Try to gather all the information you need. Ask and ask – and you'll get wiser about life in Otherland.

HOW TO FIND A FRIEND

Listen to a conversation between the fox and a lonesome prince. The prince once lived on a faraway star but is now on earth. They're now both sitting under a tree.

'Ahum,' says the prince. 'I really should get going, discovering everything, meeting people. Making friends.'

'That will be rather more difficult than you expect,' says the fox. 'People are rather busy. They like to buy their things in a supermarket ready-made. But you cannot buy friends there. So people have no friends. Making friends takes time. You know what? I want to be your friend. Just tame me.'

'How do I tame you?' asks the prince. 'How on earth does one do that?'

'You need lots of time and much patience,' answers the fox. 'First sit on the grass some distance from me. I will give you some stealthy looks. Don't say anything, that's important. Words lead to misunderstandings. And every day return here and sit in the grass with me, every day a little closer, but still without words.'

The next day the little prince showed up again. And the next, too, and many days after that. That way they grew to be friends.

'But I have a secret,' said the fox when he left at last. 'It is only with your heart that you can really see well. What is real is invisible to the eyes.' And he disappeared into the dark wood. (Inspired by *The Little Prince* by A. de St-Exupéry)

Making friends. Taming people. Everyone does this in his own way. 'With few words and by looking with your heart' is the fox's advice. I've seen many friendships grow that way among students who didn't speak the same language at all. It really works. But a country's customs may interfere here, too.

Here are some examples of 'making friends'.

SOME EXAMPLES

* 'What are their names, these friends you've been playing with in the hotel swimming pool for days now,' asks the grandmother of her 7-year-old granddaughter in Costa Rica.

'I don't know,' her granddaughter answers. 'They're new friends now. The names will come later!'

* 'Maybe that was the most difficult thing, that I had no one around me who looked like me. I kept feeling different, a stranger, not making any friends.' A white American child in Mexico.

* 'Should I wait till they ask me to join in the game? Or do I just hop in? I guess I'd better hop in or I'll never have friends here.' An observation of a Turkish girl, new in the Netherlands.

* 'Actually, I "emigrated" a long time ago within my own country from a village to the city. Then I had to fight as well to make friends.' A senior emigrant, looking back to his youth.

NAMES OF MY NEW FRIENDS

When you think you want to make friends with someone, you'll eventually ask for her name. Some people think this is important. In Otherland names might be difficult to remember, as they can be totally unfamiliar. So write it down or ask your friend to write it herself.

Here's a list for all these new names. There's room for snapshots, too.

LIST OF THE NAMES OF MY NEW FRIENDS

PICTURE

Name: ....
Address: ....
City/Town: ....
Telephone number: ....
E-mail: ....

Name: ....
Address: ....
City/Town: ....
Telephone number: ....
E-mail: ....

PICTURE

PICTURE

Name: ....
Address: ....
City/Town: ....
Telephone number: ....
E-mail: ....

PICTURE	Name: .... Address: .... City/Town: .... Telephone number: .... E-mail: ....
Name: .... Address: .... City/Town: .... Telephone number: .... E-mail:	PICTURE
PICTURE	Name: .... Address: .... City/Town: .... Telephone number: .... E-mail: ....

These names can come in handy when you need them – for doing homework, playing, parties. Maybe you can borrow a camera, so you can add pictures. That will be fun later on, too, so you can remember what it was like here in Otherland. What an adventure!

Now you've come to the end of chapter 3. Here's a short list of the contents, to make it easy when you're browsing later on.

A SHORT LIST

You're much wiser now, you know that:

* you can influence situations in your life,

* finding support is important,

* you can do this by finding friends,

* friends are made with your heart and with few words,

* this takes patience and time,

* if you want to find friends you have to get going.

This last item is what the next chapter is all about.

Here's a page for your diary. This is where you can write down all the things you don't want to forget, as you did in the other chapters.

You can also plan how you're going to make your new friends. Your family may have useful ideas as well. Don't forget to ask them.

MY DIARY

Chapter 4

Do-it-yourself

In the previous chapter you learned about communicating with others. You read what you yourself can do to fit into Otherland: be inventive, find a friend and explore. In this chapter you'll find what else you can do to get used to living in Otherland.

MY HOBBY

It helps when you remember what you really liked to do back in your home country. Something when you're involved in a hobby you even forget what time it is.

Maybe your hobbies are drawing and painting, or playing football? Or do you prefer swimming or collecting stamps? Or is it music, chess, gymnastics, baseball or judo? Or reading? There are too many hobbies to mention them all, but the question is this: can you enjoy your hobby in Otherland, somewhere nearby? Try to find out, keep on asking, because your particular hobby – .... – is something you'd really like to start doing again.

There's some space here for you to be creative. Draw or paint or make a paper collage of yourself involved with your hobby.

MY HOBBY

Is this what you really like to do? Can it be done anywhere near where you live? Then be brave and try to join others who are enjoying the same hobby or sport. Your family will certainly help you find a club, or lessons, or whatever you like. You may even find a new pastime. Otherland has lots of possibilities! This way you'll meet other kids and enjoy yourself. Later you might even introduce others to your hobby. How about forming a group to play baseball or cricket?

After you've given this some thought and have an idea about what suits you, make a plan. Keep a record of what happens. Even if it's a flop, jot it all down – including why it didn't work out.

SEARCHING FOR MY HOBBY

....

....

....

....

....

....

....

....

....

....

....

....

....

....

STILL MORE

Now you know how to grow roots – new roots as well as the roots you have in your family and your history.

* You're inventive.
* You search for friends.
* You try to adapt yourself as much as you can.
* You try to pick and choose a hobby.
* And you still have your little poems ready to steer your thinking.

That's quite a list. But there's still more to come. This is really some book you're making! Bravo, good for you!

YOUR OWN ATTITUDE

Growing new roots and feeling at home involves your own attitude, your own way of thinking. Be inventive like Puss-in-Boots. Do what Alice in Wonderland did: don't judge and keep on asking. Keep remembering to change your perspective. There are many sides to everything. You certainly haven't seen them all.

All of this – along with your willingness to adapt yourself and to explore unknown things without calling them stupid – is part of your attitude, your mindset. How do you look at the world?

AN EXPERIMENT

Now test your own attitude by carrying out an experiment you can do yourself. Measure your own mindset. What you need is a glass. Fill it halfway with water. Just half – no more and no less. This is important. Put it on a table, take a chair and sit down. Now take a good, long look at that glass of water. Observe it. What do you see? Is your glass half full or half empty? What do you see, and what do you think?

If you see a glass half full, focus on the nice clear water inside it – water that you'll still be able to drink later on, when you're thirsty. Well done! This is a helpful attitude for making yourself feel at home in your new surroundings. You could also say you're an optimist. 'Always look at the sunny side of the street'.

If you see the glass half empty, you're probably thinking about what's gone. You were so thirsty and the water was so delicious – and now only half of it is left. What a pity! You could say you're a pessimist. Now focus again on the glass and try to see it the other way round, as half full. That way you can look forward to what's still in store for you. It's a much easier way to live – and that's a promise.

It is possible to change your mindset, to steer your thoughts into a more optimistic direction. It's not easy. Just make up your mind that you can do it. You'll see for yourself – life is much easier if you see it from an optimistic frame of mind. And this is certainly one of the secrets of living a good life in Otherland. This experiment is fun to do with your family. You'll be surprised by the results!

EXPLORING

Now that you've got a more optimistic attitude, it's time to get going. Be curious, start exploring, open your eyes wide and learn. Check with your parents to find out what you're allowed to do and what you're absolutely not allowed to do. Certain things may not be allowed. It all depends on the country you're living in. It also might depend on whether you're a boy or a girl. You may not like it, but you can't close your eyes to reality. Do whatever you can and whatever you like, as long you're safe.

Every part of the world has its own dangers and risks. You're more familiar with the dangers you grew up with, the dangers of your home country: traffic, swimming in lakes or rivers or in the sea or the ocean. You knew which places were dangerous to play in. In your home country you probably knew what was allowed and what wasn't. Now there may be completely different risks: snakes, bacteria, even kidnapping, to mention just a few. Find out where the risks are. Listen to the people who care and who know the country – even if it's someone as surprising as Puss-in-Boots.
Stop, and look, listen and learn. Do you still remember?
Here are some examples to give you an idea of what to watch out for.

EXAMPLES

In the tropics you should be careful to stay out of the sunshine. Beware of overheated playground equipment. A hot slide can give you blisters. Touch it first before using it. McDonald's even puts up signs to warn the kids. Walking around barefoot outside is a no-no too! Scorpions and snakes hide in the grass in some places. There may be alligators and crocodiles where people are swimming, even in the ocean if there are swamps nearby. Beware. Getting soaking wet is very unhealthy in the tropics. And if you're still playing outside at around 6 o'clock, it's time run inside. Night and darkness fall much more quickly than in northern areas. These risks are well known to children who have been living in the tropics, but you can learn quickly, too.

In northern climates there's a big difference between summer and winter temperatures. You really have to dress accordingly, and that means warm coats, mittens, boots, scarves and warm hats. Frostbite is no fun! Summer nights can be fun for playing outdoors until it's late in the slowly fading light. You might even forget to stop and get ready for bed. Your parents won't forget, though! Here, too, the kids who have always lived here know what the risks are when it comes to safe swimming and safe skating, to mention just a few.

Traffic is dangerous in every country – and not only for children. Watch out!
The traffic rules may be different. It might be more crowded, or maybe there's a bigger mixture of things on the roads – animals, bicycles, cars, vans and buses, all mixed

up together. They may even be moving on the opposite side of the road! This really requires adjustment and a different way of looking. Before stepping out onto the road, look to the right, then to the left and then to the right again. Maybe you're used to looking left, right and left again before crossing the road. If they drive on a different side of the road compared to what you were used to, you'll have to un-learn an old habit before disciplining yourself to the new traffic rules. That's hard, but safety first...

DISCOVERING

When you are wandering through Otherland (if you're allowed), *it's time to look and stop, look and use your brains.*

There's a lot you can learn this way, just by looking.

* In shops and markets are the prices final or are you supposed to haggle?
* Do the buses run on time or 'on their own time'? Does the bus just come when it comes?
* Do people greet each other by kissing (and how many times?), hugging, shaking hands or just nodding?
* Do boys and girls play together? All the time, at certain times, or simply never?
* At birthdays, do you unwrap your presents or do you just accept them, say thank you, and open them later?

* When married people walk together does one walk behind the other or do they walk side by side?
* And where do the children walk when they have an outing with their parents?
* In shops, do people wait their turn? Do they wait in line?
* How do parents discipline their children in public?

For sure you find answers to these questions. Write them down in the next empty section. If you have more observations, jot them down as well.

MY DISCOVERIES

My discoveries:

* prices of goods in shops and markets ....
* buses ....
* greetings ....
* children ....
* presents ....
* parents ....
* their children ....
* in shops ....
* disciplining children ....

....

* and me, too ....

....

....

BE YOURSELF

After seeing all these new things, one thought may cross your mind every now and then: 'Is this for real? Am I really experiencing this? Isn't it some kind of dream?' This is part of your new life in Otherland. In the meantime you are who you are – yourself.

Do you remember your 'me mobile'? How you drew a picture of yourself in chapter 2? You – a foreign child in Otherland. A child who learned how to be herself back in her homeland, at home in her family and in her own school. As you relate to the people in Otherland, just stay as you are. You may not speak the language well, but you have other ways to communicate: gestures, facial expressions, laughing, smiling and crying. This is how you used to communicate with people before you could talk. It worked well, and you did it until you were about two years old. Here in Otherland you can make it work again, since you already have experience making yourself understood. Don't be shy. You weren't shy when you were two, were you? In the beginning it'll feel strange, speaking without words, but that doesn't matter. Don't forget to let people know how much you really appreciate them. People like to be appreciated, all over the world.

And keep in mind the little poem:

I am who I am,
said the fox.
I am who I am,
said the hare.
We are aware
no one's the boss!

I'm tall, you're small
said the fox to the hare,
be aware.
No one could call
us the same!

Yes, all of us are different.
To me it's just excellent,
forever and always to be,
just me!

TO REMEMBER

As you experience new things, and as you do so many things for the first time, don't forget: making mistakes is not bad or stupid. Mistakes teach you something: they teach you how not to. Anyway, you're young, and when you're young making mistakes isn't such a big deal.
And when you mess up completely – so what! There's usually a next time! Make it clear that you really didn't know and that you'll try to improve. You can even do that without words. It works like that in school, too. This is something we'll deal with in the next chapter. But you've learned so much already that life is sure to turn out much better than you expected.
Now you've come to the end of chapter 4. Here's a short list of the contents, to make it easy when you're browsing later on.

A SHORT LIST

You're much wiser now, at the end of chapter 4. You know that:

* the sooner you feel at home in Otherland the better,
* finding a hobby is an important help,
* your own attitude is a good support as well,
* this means being able to survive without many words,
* it's better to have a glass that's half full than one that's half empty,
* you have to change perspective,
* you can stay true to yourself and be who you are,
* people like it when you express your feelings of pleasure,
* making mistakes is no big deal.

This last item is what the next chapter is all about.

Here's a page for your diary. This is where you can write down all the things you don't want to forget. You can also plan how you're going to make new friends in school. Your family may have useful ideas as well. Don't forget to ask them.

MY DIARY

Chapter 5

School

In this chapter we'll talk about choosing schools in Otherland and about how kids in schools behave differently. You'll get advice on how to get through your first days in a new school with only a little knowledge of the new language.

CHOICES

At a certain point the day arrives: you have to go back to school. A new school. Maybe you had a little time to get yourself settled in a bit. But now there are new things to learn. Your parents have chosen a school for you. Maybe you had a say in choosing the school, too. This isn't an easy thing to do in Otherland. You have to pay attention to many different things. Should you pick an international or a local national school? A school in your neighborhood or one far away that you have to get to by school bus or daily parental taxi service?

QUESTIONS

There are many more questions to be asked:

* is everything taught in the national language or in English, German, French or Spanish?
* will you have lessons in your native language? In school, at home or not at all?
* are the teachers qualified? Sometimes this is a necessary question.
* what kind of teaching material is used? Just photocopied material or books?
* how many students are there per class?
* how are classes taught? Everybody facing front, working in groups, independent study?
* does school discipline correspond with home discipline?
* is the school modern or old-fashioned, according to your parents?
* are the teachers experienced in teaching kids from other countries? Do they speak different languages as well?

Answers to these questions will help in choosing the right school for you. But sometimes there's nothing to choose: maybe there's just one school, or maybe there's no school at all. This also happens sometimes. In that case you'll be taught at home. The school will consist of one pupil: you! Or maybe your brothers and sisters as well.

Once you know which school you'll be attending, make a drawing or look for a picture in your 'archive' of your old school in your home country. Then add a new drawing or picture of this new building, your new school. Do you see many differences? Observe!

MY OLD SCHOOL

MY NEW SCHOOL

MORE INFORMATION

You can find more information on choosing schools in the excellent publications listed at the end of this book. It's all there, titles and authors. That's not what this chapter is all about, though. Here the focus is on you and how you will experience those first weeks in your new school.

FIRST DAY OF SCHOOL - AGAIN

Do you remember the first time you went to school, way back when you were small? All alone? You were left by yourself in a group of children, and you didn't known any of them? A lot of people keep those memories for a long time. You seem to have managed pretty well! And you'll manage just as well now. With your little knowledge of the language you'll be all on your own in a new situation. If the language is familiar to you you'll realize how lucky you are. But even then, it's still a challenge.

First of all, keep remembering not to be a shy hare. When the people who are familiar to you have left and you're on your own – be brave and face the challenge.

Take a good look at your surroundings and be alert. See what's happening and what is expected of you. Act accordingly. Don't be afraid of making mistakes!

Sometimes the director of the school will want to talk with you before you are introduced to the others. Usually your new teacher will get to know you a bit, and after that you'll meet the kids of your new group.

You may have to take some tests first so the school can measure your knowledge of certain subjects. Do your best, and show them what you know! You have quite a lot to show, since you speak your own language fluently.

Be proud of that, no matter what difficult things you may have to do. You may have other qualities as well. It's like the boy who had been living in a desert country.
He was having a hard time learning the new language, and he said to his teacher:
'Learning this language is hard, but I know how to ride with five camels!'
So keep up your self-confidence.

At last, when everything is settled, you'll go to your group. Now comes the next challenge. You look for a seat, or one is given to you. You sit down and look around, thinking: 'What's going to happen next?'

NEW BEHAVIOR

Now you've got to try to find out the following things:

* how do students address teachers? What do they call their teacher?
* how does a student indicate that he wants to say something? How does he draw the teacher's attention?
* does the teacher speak a bit of English as well, if you're in a non-English-speaking culture?
* are you allowed to use your English in the classroom?

* may you ask for a different seat if, say, you want to sit next to a friend? Remember, finding a friend is very important!
* do the students stand up when a teacher or the director enters the classroom?
* are you allowed to consult with a friend during lessons, or to work together in small groups? This is especially important for you as you struggle without much knowledge of the language;
* do the students get out of their seats without asking permission?
* do the students obey the teacher immediately?

Look, observe and imitate. But use your brains. Imitate the required behavior. This is how you learned when you were very young: by listening, looking and then imitating. If you don't understand, ask!

To help you reflect on these challenging first days in your new school, here's an opportunity to write down the answers to the above questions. And to write down anything else you need to keep in mind, of course.

IN MY NEW CLASSROOM

In my new classroom the students sometimes do things differently than I'm used to.

Here's what I see them doing:

....

....

....

....

....

....

But many things they do are just what students do in my home country. Some of these things are:

....

....

....

....

....

....

I've also learned that:

My teacher is called ....

My school friend's name is ....

The other kids I hang out with are ....

....

....

In the classroom we're allowed to ....

....

and to ....

But it's strictly forbidden to ....

....

I've also observed that ....

....

....

....

Are you amazed by many things? No wonder! Just share them ....

....

....

....

....

....

....

....

....

Another thing that might be new to you is wearing a uniform – or not wearing a uniform, if that's what you were used to. In both cases it feels strange. The advantage of a uniform is that you don't have to decide what to wear to school in the morning. When all the kids wear uniforms they're also more alike. But look-alikes make it harder for you. There's no distinction between those who wear expensive clothes and those who don't. You don't have to worry about whether you're wearing the right outfit.

WHAT'S YOUR NAME?

Of course you'd like to remember the names of the kids you play with. It's very annoying if you don't remember the names of your new friends, on top of all the other words you don't know yet. So what do you do?

You add names and addresses plus phone numbers to the address list you started in chapter 3. This really is a great help, since you often find yourself forgetting unfamiliar names in the beginning. In Vietnam, for example, the names of students could be Vu Hong, Nguyen Minh Ho, Nguyen Cua and Vu Van Khanh. Last names come first. It's quite a job telling them apart. On the other hand, it's not easy for Vietnamese to adapt to the Western system, either.

When you hang out with them, you call them Hong, Ho, Cua and Khanh, although we can't tell by their names whether they're boys or girls. In other countries you might have different problems. But you'll get used to it rather quickly. Just pay attention.

Your name may sound strange or unfamiliar to other people as well. You come to understand this after reading the paragraph in chapter 2 about different perspectives and turning the tables!

However, it will be easier for your new fellow students because all they have to remember is one name – yours. It's unusual for many foreign students to come into a new classroom at the same time. But you have many names to learn.

Many children in the world, all of them in their own Otherland, have to live through these exhausting first days in their new schools. You can read some of their stories in the following parts of letters and diaries. They were written by children about their school days in Otherland. How different these experiences can be!

BITS AND PIECES

'The only thing you can do is sit and look around, since you don't understand a word they're saying. I didn't connect with Dutch girls because I didn't speak Dutch. I had landed in a completely different world. My freedom in Morocco was actually much greater.'
A Moroccan girl, 12 years old, about her school in the Netherlands.

'Then I keep on thinking: Am I making mistakes with my English, is it good enough? I know the answers all right, but how do I make myself understood?'
A Dutch boy, 11 years old, about his education in the USA.

'I sometimes feel ashamed for my home when I'm in school. At home I wear different clothes. I take different food with me to school. I can do things at school that I'm not allowed to do at home, like behaving like a macho. Sometimes it's just the other way round: playing with girls. When you do that in school you're laughed at. They call you a sissy!'
A 10-year-old German boy in Costa Rica.

'In my class are just English-speaking girls with the white skin of evil.'
A 9-year-old girl from Mali in the UK.

'When you have to speak a different language you always feel stupid in the beginning. Everyone thinks you're more stupid in school, too.'
A Canadian girl, 12 years old, about her school in France.

'In the beginning I had a hard time. But then I made friends with someone and things got better. The teacher always helped me. I've been in school six months now. It's just an American school and I like it. I like it even better than back in my home country. I'm doing fine.'
A Dutch student in Australia, 11 years old.

'I'm in Yokohoma International School, a very cool school with more than 400 students. More than 30 nationalities are represented here. It's fun. We have a lot of different subjects here, including the Japanese language. Last year I lived in Thailand, where there was a Dutch school. Now all the classes are in English. Sometimes that's very difficult. But it's getting better and better because I have a very cool teacher who teaches English very well. Once a week we have Dutch lessons given by a nice Dutch teacher. I like those lessons too.'
A Dutch student in Japan, 12 years old.

And now, what are you going to write?

MY FIRST DAY IN MY NEW SCHOOL

HOME SCHOOL

What if no school can be found for you? What happens then? There are hundreds of kids in this situation all over the world. These kids are students of the 'world schools' – schools that send lesson packets to kids abroad by mail, internet, e-mail or fax.

In a quiet corner of your home a place is set aside for you to study in - your school. That's where you do your lessons at home, just like in school. The difference is that your teachers are your parents or family friends. You can find the addresses of these world education centers on the internet.

When you enroll in a school like this, you invent a nice new name for it. Write it on a piece of wood, paper or cardboard. Decorate your sign and hang it in your new school. Now you'll never forget you're in school, not just at home.
One thing here is certain: you speak, learn and are taught in your own language.

In the next chapter you'll get a preview of Otherland words, which are handy to know when you're new in school.

But first, here's a short list of the contents of chapter 5.

A SHORT LIST

Now you know how to:

* find the information necessary to make a choice of schools,

* survive the first days in a new school,

* remember the unusual names of classmates,

* join in lessons by imitating correct group behavior,

* create your own home school.

Here's the next page for your diary. This is where you can write down all the things you don't want to forget, as you did in the other chapters.

MY DIARY

Chapter 6

In the classroom

Whatever school you end up attending, you'll have to follow the lessons – sports, art and many more subjects, some of them quite new to you. As soon as you're in school, you'll be faced with questions about these lessons.

HOW DO I READ THIS?

There will be reading books and exercise books, of course, and they may be written in a language you hardly understand. People write their thoughts down in many different ways. Just look at the following lines written in all kind of different languages. This is a copy of a page from Peter Spier's book.

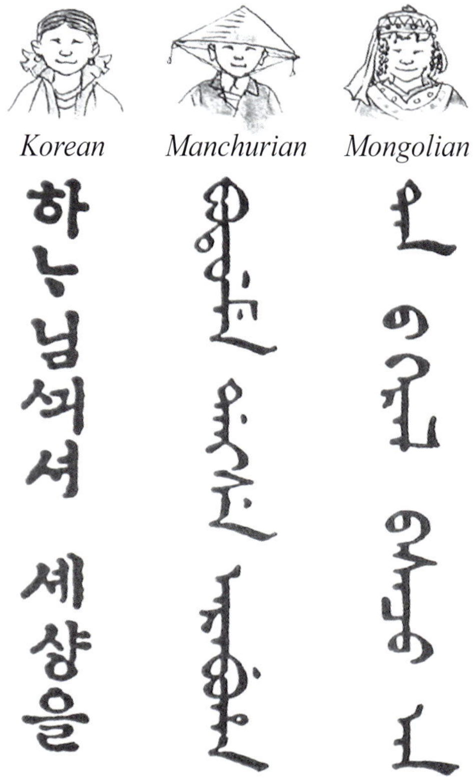

Here you can see that you're lucky if the books you'll be studying from are in an alphabet you can read. In most cases, however, you can't understand what's written down. It's even more difficult when the words are written from top to bottom, as they do in the Far East. Look at the following lines.

So far I haven't even mentioned the books read the other way round. The beginning of the book is at what we call the back. In those books it's called the front, and the end comes at what we call beginning. This is done in the Middle East. All these scripts look like cryptography – secret writing – to us. And people who live in

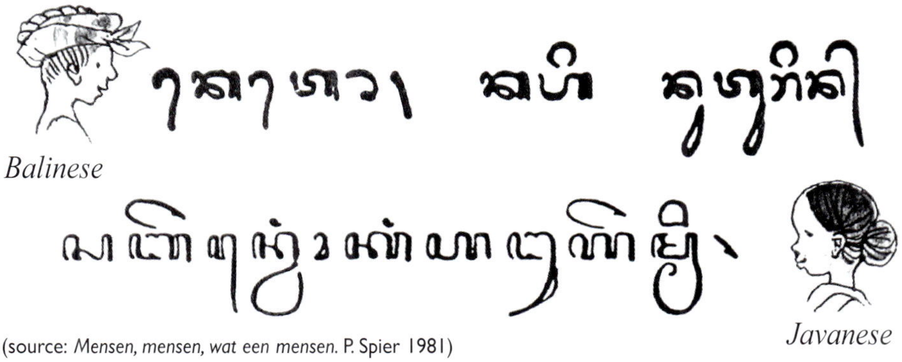

(source: *Mensen, mensen, wat een mensen.* P. Spier 1981)

those secret alphabet countries would probably think the same of our writing if you were to bring one of your textbooks to school.

Do you remember what you read in chapter 2 about different perspectives? About turning the tables, the topsy-turvy world? The end of a book can also be the beginning. But this shouldn't surprise you. You're prepared. You know that different can be normal.

HOW DO I LEARN?

Maybe you learned some easy words in Otherlandish, maybe before you went to Otherland. Now you can use those words, and of course you'll be learning new ones very quickly. No need to go to school for that. One of the secrets of Otherland is that you'll learn more words and you'll start speaking the language sooner by playing with Otherland kids! Fortunately you've already started your search for friends! In school you'll learn the school language and how to write it correctly.

Now is the time to learn some words in advance that you'll need in the classroom. To do this you need the help of someone who knows both English and Otherlandish. This could be a parent, a teacher or someone else who can do the translation for you. It's very important for you to have these words in your vocabulary in the classroom. It will help you to follow the lessons more quickly and to express your thoughts.

MY NEW WORDS

English	Otherlandish
first	....
last	....
next	....
bottom	....
top	....
middle	....
front	....
back	....
near	....
far	....
OK/well done	....
wrong	....
take	....

begin ....
get ready ....
write ....
read ....
do ....
make ....
listen ....
say ....
talk ....
sit ....
leave/go away ....
run ....
stop ....
repeat ....
compare ....
look like ....
go to ....
book ....
notebook ....
page ....
pencil ....
pen ....
paper ....
homework ....
home/house ....
school ....
break ....
food ....
sports ....

It seems a long list, but it makes an enormous difference if you know these words. It's easier to understand what's happening around you and to know what you're expected to do. And it's easier to follow the lessons – it's even easier to use some of them yourself.

WHAT I MEAN TO SAY

After you've learned the list of words above, the following important short sentences or expressions are next. They help you deal with the amazing difference between 'not knowing' and 'not understanding the question', between knowing the answer but not being able to find the right words. You'll feel less stupid if you can say that you know the answer but don't know the words in Otherlandish to say it.
This makes it easier both for you and the teacher, so if you can't give the answer to a question the teacher will know why. You'll enjoy learning more because it feels better.

THE NECESSARY SENTENCES

	Otherlandish
I don't understand	....
I don't know	....
What does it mean?	....
Please speak slowly	....
Please repeat this	....
I know the answer	....
I don't know the word for it	....
Where is?	....
What's its name?	....
This is new to me	....
May I do this again?	....
What's the reason? / Why?	....
How about that!	....

Once you know how to use the sentences in the classroom along with the words you've learned, you'll really be getting there! It's great if the people at home can help you out. The beginning of a new period in school is always hard.
You can also practice with your brothers and sisters, if you have any here and they're starting school, too. If you have a school in your own home, though, you don't need this kind of practice. But the sentences and words might come in handy for music lessons or sports. If not, just skip it!

TRICKS

Every day you'll be learning words now, little by little, just a few each day – like brushing your teeth. This is a piece of your secret of Otherland, too. You need these words to feel at home in Otherland and to be happy at school. In the beginning there are many, many words you don't know, no matter how hard you study. Even if you're doing your best you may get depressed! After studying a language for many years you still come across new and unknown words. But there are tricks to help you make good guesses, use common sense and make your brains work. Don't stop and panic at unknown or unfamiliar words. Keep thinking, keep guessing. Here's what I mean.

EXAMPLE

Imagine you're in a classroom. The teacher starts a lesson about the zoo. He starts by saying: 'I was in the zoo the other day, and what did I see? Elephants, tigers and doinies! The doinies were roaring as if they were terribly hungry. They kept pacing back and forth in their cages and growling. They shook their manes and scratched the sand with their front paws.'

In this story you don't know the word *doinies*'. You're doing fine if you understand the gist of the lesson. You might panic and say to yourself: 'I don't know this. I'll never be able to answer the teacher's questions. I'll never learn this language'.

But if you keep on thinking and using your common sense, you'll find that you know a lot about the doinie:

* it's kept in the zoo;
* there's probably more than one of them;
* most likely it's an animal;
* a doinie is not an elephant or a tiger;
* it has a mane, four legs, it scratches and roars.

You'll conclude that a doinie is a .... Later you could check in a dictionary if you're still not sure. Of course you can always ask, too. But as you can see, you can do a lot by making good use of your brains. Don't panic and don't give up.
Think of it as a guessing game, and put this trick in your box of secrets.

STILL MORE TRICKS

In every society people talk together and tell each other stories. They often write them down as well, and they do it in their own language. But they write their stories in their own special way. You don't see this immediately. You only notice it in your reaction to a story. It seems boring to you – too long or too detailed. Maybe there doesn't seem to be any point to the story. Maybe there's too much going on and it doesn't seem to have a strong direction, so you can't really get into it.
This reaction is caused by the fact that you're not used to this way of communicating, of telling a story. Ever since you were very young you've been listening to the people around you use a different language and a different style of talking and storytelling. When you tell a story you mention the important parts in the beginning and the rest follows. Look at some of the familiar fairy tales that are always built on this pattern.

'Once upon a time there was a .... And this .... Then along came ....' You were probably told these stories when you were little, so this is how you listen when you're in school. That's how you read stories. You aren't aware of this, you just do it. But now, in a different language, in a different culture, the long part of the story may come first. You may wonder: 'What's all this about? What on earth do they mean?' And eventually you get to the heart of the matter. Of course it could also be the other way around. You look for the heart of the story in the wrong place.
Some people can't concentrate that long. They get irritated or bored. This feeling is the signal that stories or jokes are based on different patterns.
In school this means paying extra attention. You've got to be more alert. Keep asking yourself: 'Where is the important part, what's the heart?'
You'll be able to use this way of paying attention and being cautious whenever you communicate in your Otherland. The pattern is always hidden, but it's very important.

Another trick is not to let others rush you. Think before you answer. Take your time. You need a bit more time because you have to put your answer together in a different way. Don't hesitate to explain this to your teachers, or ask your parents to do so. The longer you're in Otherland, the faster you'll be able to speak. You'll even be able to make jokes! But in the beginning it makes you very tired. So make sure you get plenty of sleep, if you need it...

FORGET ME NOT

This is quite a lot of things not to forget. How do you keep your head from turning into a sieve? Imagine that you put all these pieces of your secret of Otherland in a box – including all the tricks. It's your box of tricks and secrets. You might even write all these difficult words and sentences on separate cards and put them in a real little box. On one side you write in English and on the other you write the same thing in Otherlandish. Once you know the translation from one side to the other, without peeking, you really know the word and you can get rid of it. This requires training and perseverance.

On the other hand, by the time you've written all the words down on both sides of the cards and put everything in your box, you'll know most of the words already. That's another little trick!

A SHORT LIST

In this chapter you learned:

* many new Otherlandisch words,

* new ways of listening and reading,

* not to panic in trying to understand difficult unknown words,

* how to use a guessing game in solving a riddle.

Try to remember what you learned in the preceding chapters. Go back and browse through the last pages of each chapter by going to 'A short list'.
If it's helpful you could put the 'short list' lines on cards as well.
Don't forget the little poem. So far it's been very important.

Not knowing
what to do,
or where to turn?
Stop and look,
listen and learn.

Not knowing
what to do,
where's the link?
Stop and look,
listen and think.

Still don't know?
What a difficult task!
Stop and look,
listen and ask.

The next chapter is all about fun things: family, friends, visiting and parties – your life outside your school.

Here's a page for your diary. This is where you can write down all the things you don't want to forget – your questions and comments.
You can add pictures and drawings, too, just as you did in the other chapters.
Need more space, use a scrapbook!

MY DIARY

Chapter **7**

Friends, family and festivities

This is a chapter to help you forget about school. Here we'll talk about some of the other adventures that you might have in Otherland.

FRIENDS

Now that you've made some new friends it's nice to know a little bit more about the way they live. How they celebrate their holidays. How their families relate to each other. About the games the children play. About quarreling and making up again.
In each country in the world these things might be very different. You'll appreciate being prepared for all the differences.

In this book you won't find lists of do's and don'ts for each country. It would take a complete book to hold them all. Even then your country might be missing.
No, in this book it's up to you, notice where you have to pay attention, just as you did before. You'll see where the behavior is different, and why, and how this might involve you. You'll learn to change your own perspective and to react differently – if necessary.

When your friends welcome you into their lives, you play together and maybe you even visit their homes. This is the time to have on hand the scrapbook you made of your homeland. You can show your new friends the parts about your old school, your house and your neighborhood. You may even have some extra pictures. It will help you let them know who you are and where you come from. They'll fill in the words you may not know yet.

COME AND PLAY WITH ME?

Just think how happy you'll be when you're asked to come and play for the first time in Otherland. Happy – and a little fearful at the same time. What will it be like there, you wonder. If the kids are your own nationality you won't expect it to be much different than when you played with friends in your home country. You're used to those situations. But what about Otherland friends and their families, or playing in the homes of other foreign children? What happens then?

Then you'll do what you discovered earlier in your book. You'll watch your friend and do what he does. Be friendly. If you don't know many words when you go to your friend's house, just say 'hello' or 'ola' or whatever the greeting is in this country. Everyone will understand this, and they'll also understand that you're not fluent in Otherlandish yet. There are many, many different ways of greeting people in the world, as the illustration shows.
Which one is right for your Otherland?

People greet one another by:

* kissing, sometimes even three times: left cheek, right cheek, left cheek again – starting on the right or the left;
* hugging and patting backs at the same time;
* shaking both hands fiercely at the same time;
* shaking hands at arms length while looking each other in the eyes;
* bowing at some distance; how deeply you bow conveys a meaning;
* nodding;
* lifting your hat;
* saluting, among soldiers;
* waving and shouting, calling a greeting;
* saying 'hello', 'hi', 'good morning' etc.

These are just a few of the ways that people greet you, show they recognize you, let you know you're welcome, that they're happy to meet with you – or just acknowledge your existence.

ADJUSTING

In greeting others you start by imitating the ways of your friends. Sometimes it's very hard to adjust yourself to the habits of a new land. Vietnamese kids have problems at first greeting older people, like their teacher, when they're on their bicycles. Just calling out 'Hello, master' and waving is very rude to them. This is how they were taught to act. In Holland this kind of greeting is considered normal friendly behavior. It's rude not to greet your teacher this way. Because the Vietnamese kids are also in Holland now, they start greeting people in the Dutch way after a while. They adjust themselves and adopt new habits.

This could happen to you as well. You might find new ways of greeting strange at first, but by adjusting yourself you'll acquire new habits.
In fact, that's the way it usually works with new habits. In the beginning it doesn't feel good, but you'll end up doing as the Romans do – because you're in Rome. You're the guest here. Some people who have just arrived in a new land expect Otherlanders to adapt themselves to them. In the long run this doesn't work and it often causes many problems.

Do you remember how it was in your home country? Didn't you expect others to act like you?

EATING TOGETHER

The more often you visit your friend's home and the more you enjoy being there, the more you'll get to know family life in Otherland from the inside. Of course it's only one family, but still it might open your eyes to the differences.

* Do they eat their meals sitting together, listening to each others' stories at least once a day? Or do they 'graze', taking whatever they like out of the fridge whenever they feel like it?

* Does the mother of the family prepare the meal with the girls in the kitchen and serve the food to the father and the boys, while not joining them to eat?

* Do they use plates? Knives, forks and spoons? If not – stop, watch and imitate! You could eat chicken and rice with your fingers and crab with a hammer, but what about soup? Just drink it! In some countries you should gulp when you drink or they'll think you don't like it.

* Do they empty their plates, or do they always leave a little food?

* When you finish your drink does it mean you want more? And do they immediately fill up your glass again? Or is it a sign that you've had your fill? If the first is the custom, leave some of your drink in the glass or cup if you don't like it that much or you're not thirsty anymore.

* Does burping after eating a meal mean you're complimenting the cook? Then it's rude not to burp. Or does it mean that you're ill mannered? Then it is rude to burp.

* Are you allowed to talk during the meal? Sometimes this is considered ill-mannered.

If you'd like to cook in the Otherland way, check out in information to see if you can find something nice in the international cookbooks for kids. Or check your local bookstore.

WELL MANNERED?

As you read in the paragraph above, every country in the world has its own manners – table manners, manners for greeting, manners for living together. Good manners in one country may be bad manners in another. This shouldn't surprise you any more, now that you know about the change of perspective. Don't worry about using the wrong manners. You're young and can make mistakes. Just apologize. No one will really worry. Maybe it worries you, though. If it does, think of the little poem *Stop and look, listen and learn, over and over again,* including in the home of your friends.

Now write about the first time you ate out in Otherland, and maybe add a photograph later on. Did you like it? Was it an adventure? Or was it not so different from meals in your own home? It's nice to keep a record of this for later, when you're back home again or living in another country. Things like this are soon forgotten!

MY FIRST TIME EATING WITH FRIENDS

....

....

....

....

....

....

....

....

....

....

PLAYING TOGETHER

Things may be different when you're playing with your friends, too. Be prepared to be alert and try to find out the answers to the following questions:

* Will you mostly play outdoors or indoors?
* Does each kid have his own toys?
* Are you allowed to do the same things there that you do at home?
* Who's the leader? The person whose house you're playing?
* Do all the kids join in?
* Who cleans up the toys when it's time to go home?

* Are the games you play the same as the ones you played in your homeland? With the same rules? It's really complicated when you're playing 'hide and seek' with different rules and you don't know what they are. Then you really have to pay attention and adapt – and have fun at the same time.

* When playing inside, how do they deal with doors? Do closed doors (except in bathrooms) mean you need privacy? Do they mean you're trying to be secretive? Or is it considered good manners to close all the doors behind you?

Keep your eyes open, imitate and do as they do.

All these questions are meant to ease you into Otherland family life. Once you know what to watch out for, you'll notice these things and act accordingly. That's how it works. And this way you'll enjoy life in Otherland much sooner. You'll make the difficult period shorter.

Now you can read a few little stories about playing with others.

SOME EXAMPLES

* Lucinda, 6 years old, lives in Costa Rica and for the first time goes to play with a friend who is temporarily staying with her grandmother. When her daddy picks her up after two hours playing there, she is sad. No, it wasn't nice. There were no toys, just wet black mud around the house, nothing to play with, and the TV constantly on. There were lots of other older kids who kept teasing them. And her friend just kept watching TV all the time.

Lucinda's family decides to *stop and look, listen and learn.* Then Lucinda begins to understand why her friend has so much fun playing in her home. Lucinda has wonderful toys, her friend enjoys there what she lacks at home and at her grandma's. They talk about the difference between 'having' – a nice home, a lot of toys, many clothes - and 'being' – a good friend, nice and polite.
The end of the story is that Lucinda and her friend will go on sharing her toys, and for the time being they'll play at Lucinda's house. Later on she'll visit her friend's house again and bring some nice playthings for them both to enjoy.
This worked well. A year later they were still friends and playing in both homes on a regular basis.

* Leslie, an American girl, 12 years old, goes to stay at her friend's place for a weekend. They live in Latin America. The first day is great and they have a lot of fun. But on Sunday morning she sees that her friend's sister has put on Leslie's new T shirt – she couldn't find it anywhere! – and her friend is wearing her new special hairclips. They both didn't even ask! Leslie is angry. When she starts to complain, her friend says: 'You can wear any of our things, too. We're all friends. It belongs to all of us.' Leslie has to adjust herself to this idea. She never looked at it that way before.

When Leslie is home again she talks about it with her family. In America a lot of things are your own. They belong to you or your sister or whoever. 'I' and 'mine are important words. In Peru – and other countries in the world – people own many things together. 'We' and 'our' are more important than 'I' and 'mine'. What's mine is also yours, so obviously you can use it as well. Leslie isn't angry any more. She understands what happened and will adapt herself in order to maintain the friendship. But if her friend were ever to visit her in the US she would explain her world, too!

* Mohamed, 10 years old, plays with Jan, his Dutch friend of the same age. When Mohamed says Jan's water pistol is fantastic, Jan doesn't give it to Mohamed as a present. Mohamed is disappointed and a bit sulky. He wants to go home early and tells his friend he is mean and greedy.

When a fight is about to break out, Jan's mother intervenes. She does *stop and look, listen and learn* with them. Both boys then understand that they have acted out of habit, that different customs lead to different behavior. They understand that Mohamed adapts himself when at Jan's house and Jan adapts himself when they're at Mohamed's house. 'But', says Mohamed, 'when you're at my place you may take whatever you like.' Later they come to another decision: when they're in Turkey they'll do it the way Turkish friends do. In Holland they'll do it the way Dutch friends do.

WHAT'S IMPORTANT?

These examples show how you're stuck in a web of habits, often without realizing it. These habits and customs, these ways of thinking, were formed in the family and country you grew up in.

Now have a look at the things that might be important to you or to other people from your country, or to the Otherland people.

THIS IS IMPORTANT

	row 1 To me	row 2 To someone from my country	row 3 To an Otherlander
Pocket money	....	....	....
Giving my own opinion	....	....	....
Being alone, playing by myself	....	....	....
Being different	....	....	....
Sharing	....	....	....
Playing fair	....	....	....
Having my own things	....	....	....
Caring for others	....	....	....
My family	....	....	....
Girls and boys being allowed to do the same	....	....	....

YOUR TASK

First read this list once more, very carefully. Now you're going to do three things:

1. Fill in a number in the first row. This is your opinion. The numbers range from 10 = very important, to 1 = very unimportant. So if you think pocket money is the most important item on the list, give it a 10. You give 1 to an unimportant issue. This isn't very easy to do, and the middle numbers 5, 6 and 7 are the most difficult to decide on. When you've finished this task you'll know what you find important. Read it one more time and continue with row 2.
2. Once again fill in a number, this time in the second row. You decide how important the people in your country might find this item. Do it in the same way, from 1 to 10. Try and guess the thoughts of your friends back home. Come on, do your best! Now read it again and see if your opinions are same as the opinions of your friends. Is there much of a difference?

3. In the third row decide how you think Otherland kids see the importance of these items. Use the numbers 1 to 10 again. Your Puss-in-Boots – your support in Otherland – might be a great help here.

Did you fill in all of the numbers? This was a hard task, wasn't it? But it gives you a lot of information: about yourself, your old country and your new country.
Now study the list and look for the really big differences: if you put a 4 where an Otherland kid has an 8, this is an item where there are completely different opinions and where clashes might arise. This isn't about right or wrong, or about good or bad. Do you remember chapter 3, the perspectives? This is about a different point of view. Put a big check mark next to those places where you score low and the other scored high, or the other way round. That's where the greater differences occur.

MISUNDERSTANDINGS

Of course you know that people sometimes misunderstand each other. This can also happen in your own native language. In the middle of a busy street your mother cries out 'Stop' and you think she said 'Go'. Uh oh - you just missed an accident!
In the Otherland language it is easier to 'mishear' words and misunderstand them. Not only that, but sometimes it's hard to know what the word actually means. In French, 'adieu' means good-bye forever. 'Au revoir', on the other hand, means 'see you later'. So it's easy to create a misunderstanding, even when you use simple words.
When you have a different opinion, misunderstandings can happen, too. You don't understand the other person, and you don't know exactly why. Your line of thought may not be the same as his at all. You've given all this plenty of thought and now you're wiser than many kids your age. Do you recognize the following examples and the different ways of thinking?

EXAMPLES

* You think she's coming to your party but she doesn't show up.
  The misunderstanding is this: your attitude is to say what you think. You invited her and she said: 'Yes, thank you, I'll be there'. But she knows it's very rude to say: 'No, I don't want to come', so she doesn't say what she thinks. You may think she's fooling you, she thinks she's being nice to you. Different ways of thinking.

* You're allowed to stay in school and continue your education, but your friend has to drop out. You think this is unfair, but she finds it normal.
  The misunderstanding is this: it's normal that boys and girls have the same right to education, in your opinion. According to her way of thinking boys in the family have more right to study than girls. Girls are supposed to get married and be supported by their husbands.

* While you're playing with your friend he moves off to sit by himself in his bedroom. He just wants to be by himself for a while. You think he's angry.
  The misunderstanding is this: you think being together is nicer than being on your own. He thinks just the opposite.

Now do you understand how misunderstandings occur? You're sure to have experienced them yourself. You may write them down in the next paragraph. Try to understand the underlying train of thought as well. And if something is still worrying you, talk about it with your parents, your teacher or your Puss-in-Boots. If you have no misunderstandings now, skip this part and use it later. They're certain to happen some day.

MY MISUNDERSTANDINGS

....

....

....

....

....

....

It's very difficult to understand that people – children as well – can have ideas differing from your own. We simply expect others to be like us, to think as we do. We behave like the others. Didn't we learn by imitating? Deep down in our hearts there is this feeling that everyone thinks the same way – the way I think. But you have to learn that this is not true at all: people have their own ideas. This is an important part of the secret of Otherland.
If you find this hard to understand, it's a good time to read the part **'what's important'**. You're certainly going to need it. Consult your family, too, if you come across ideas you don't understand yet.

FAMILY

In the list you filled in with numbers, you gave a number to 'family', too. That's the family you meet when you play with your friends, the ones you see at your school, and of course those at home, your own family.
You're probably familiar with the small family: father and kids, mother and kids, father and mother with kids, or two partners with kids. In the small-family world a family of five kids is considered large. Then add your aunts, uncles and cousins and your grandparents. They all have a bit of the same blood, but they don't usually live in the same house.
In other countries this can be completely different. 'Family' means more than the small family. A family lives all together: parents, grandparents, uncles, aunts and many more children. This is called a great family or extended family. And then there are the friends of the family. They may be called father, mother, aunt or uncle, brother or sister as well. Sometimes this is very confusing. They have these names because they are like family. That's their role. A family with five kids is not a large family at all in the great-family world.

Here follow some examples.

EXAMPLES OF FAMILY

* In Vietnam a boy talks to a foreign friend about his neighbor and says: ' … and he's my father'. 'He's your father?' the friend asks, very surprised to hear this. 'Well, not really my father', answers the Vietnamese boy, 'but he is like a father to me. We use these words to indicate his role. To me he acts like a father. You and I may become brothers in the future'.
* In the Netherlands a mother comes to school to enroll three new children. She already has four kids of that age group in school, so they don't differ that much in age. She calls herself their 'mother', but the children are nieces and nephews, her sister's kids, living in Surinam. Her sister's family came for a holiday and the kids were left behind to be educated by their aunt. She is their mother now.
* In Sri Lanka children are given as presents to childless members of the family. There brothers and sisters are turned into nieces and nephews.
* Sometimes, in the small-family world, good neighbors or very good friends are called 'uncle and aunt'.

These examples show that in different countries the same word can stand for different things. Like the games you play, the name is the same but the rules are different.

CELEBRATIONS

The same goes for celebrations or parties – family celebrations and national celebrations. Just think of your birthday. How do you celebrate it in your home country? Exactly the same way you celebrate it here in Otherland? Show it here. Say it's your tenth birthday.

MY BIRTHDAY

In Otherland they celebrate birthdays their own way. In some countries a birthday isn't important at all. They celebrate your saint's day instead. They do this in southern Europe. There you even celebrate two birthdays! Giving and receiving presents can also be done in different ways. Do you thank a person, accept the present and put it away unopened? Look at the way it's done in Otherland. Besides family celebrations there are also national and religious celebrations. To the people who follow a country's religion these holidays will be of great importance. At the back you'll find the title of a beautiful book on celebrations all over the world.

In the following paragraph you can write down the days that are celebrated in Otherland. Does this mean free school days, or pageants, processions and parades?

Write about it and make it more interesting and beautiful with pictures or a collage of newspaper clippings in your diary or scrapbook.

Do you notice how nice and interesting your book is now? You're doing a great job. And if you haven't celebrated any holidays in Otherland yet, skip this part and do it later when you have this information.

HOLIDAYS IN OTHERLAND

My new holidays in Otherland are: ....

....

....

How do you give and receive presents in Otherland? ....

....

....

....

Now you've come to the end of chapter 7. Here's a short list of the contents to help you memorize now and browse later.

A SHORT LIST

In this chapter you learned that:

* your Otherland friends sometimes have a completely different way of thinking,
* misunderstandings occur because you don't hear or understand someone,
* working or playing together requires cooperation and adjustment on both sides,
* habits and customs differ from country to country,
* national, religious and family celebrations may be celebrated in other ways,
* a neighbor can be family member, too!

In the next chapter we'll talk about difficult moments, about keeping the peace and about the thin line between a misunderstanding and a real quarrel.

Here's another page for your diary. This is where you can write down all the things you don't want to forget as well as your questions and remarks. You can add pictures and drawings, too, just as you did in the other chapters.

MY DIARY

Chapter **8**

Difficult moments

So far you've worked hard to grow new roots in the now not-so-unfamiliar Otherland. So far you've done well: you know so much more now than when you started your book. Just think of all the pages you've read, the drawings you've made and all the other creative activities you've done.

WHAT DO I KNOW NOW?

* You're amazed like Alice in Wonderland, but you don't judge whether things are good or bad;
* you're inventive like Puss-in-Boots;
* you're shrewd as a fox;
* you found an Otherland friend (hopefully) to help you when you need it;
* you explore, you're curious, and you're using common sense;
* you know quite a few Otherland words;
* you know how to adjust to new situations;
* you noticed that many things are the same and many things are different;
* you saw that normal in Otherland may not be what's normal to you;
* you know how to deal with difficult situations:
* *stop and look, listen and learn... and look one more time.*

TEMPERS FLARING UP

Even though you know about all these things, tempers may still flare up unexpectedly. Just imagine yourself frying eggs. You're being very careful and the eggs look delicious, mmm, when all of a sudden your frying pan bursts into flames. What a shock! You just manage to put out the fire. No harm done. The same kind of thing can happen between people: suddenly one word may give rise to a great misunderstanding. It feels like fire. You're shocked, you feel misunderstood, sad, or simply stunned.

This could happen to any of us. But certainly in your situation, where so much is new, it will happen sooner and more often. In a new situation you could easily pick the wrong words to express yourself and not have the right words to solve a problem.

Kids who are new in a country get into fights more quickly because of this lack of words. You may understand it, but it's still not right. Hitting and fighting don't solve problems, they only show who's stronger...

Cases like this usually happen because of a great misunderstanding: a conflict. A conflict may be a fight, a fierce difference of opinion, a quarrel or a serious problem – a crisis. It's always troublesome when emotions flare up and people start to fight. But this is what happens when people are living together. In the previous chapter you saw how misunderstandings can arise. Difficult moments are the result.

EXAMPLES

* In school your teacher thinks you're being fresh, while you're not aware of it at all. All you said was that you don't agree with something. This is what you're used to doing. In your old school you were even urged to act like this. But now your teacher is angry with you: a blazing fire! The result is that you lose your temper, too, and you're also sad. Anger makes you cry.

* Some boys in your neighborhood are always teasing you. All of a sudden you're fed up with them. Enough is enough. Your anger flares up and you start fighting.

* This stupid homework. Day after day – and then these extra language exercises! You're so fed up with all of it. Your anger flares up. You bang doors, throw your books in a corner and storm outside.

I bet you can think of many more crisis situations.

MY CONFLICT

....

....

....

WHAT I DID THEN

....

....

....

In these examples you read how children used their bodies to express what they couldn't say with words. Maybe you found better ways to respond to the conflicts in the examples.

Your answer to example 1 could be:

* Swallow your tears, count to 10 and think: This man has no idea what I mean. When the lesson is over I'll go to him and try to explain. A good teacher will understand your problem, and together you'll solve the conflict. If he still doesn't understand, talk it over with your parents and explain your side of the problem.

Your answer to example 2 could be:

* React to the boys. Protest in short, clear sentences, breathing deeply and standing up straight. Tell them: 'Stop it. I'm angry. I don't want this. Stop it now.' Show them who you are, make yourself tall. A clear I-message works. You'll be amazed how well

it works. In doing this you're being quite brave. Another option is to run as fast as you can! Hopefully an adult will show up in the meantime to help solve the conflict, too. Sometimes this isn't necessary at all.

Your answer to the last example could be:

* Recognize the problem, sit back and relax. Breathe deeply, close your books and put them away. Say to yourself: 'Tomorrow is another day!' Listen to your favorite music, dance to the rhythm, or play with your dog or your sister or brother.
In short, take a break and have some fun! The next day you'll be prepared to get going again. Wake up a little early, finish the job and... the problem is solved.
You're ready to go.

THE RIGHT ANSWERS

As you read over the answers in the previous examples, one thing stands out. Do you see it, too?

You're angry and you can't stop yourself from fighting. You'll never be able to stop fighting if you're angry, sad or excited. Just remember: *stop and look, listen and learn.* Calm down. Think. You can't think when you're angry. All you can do is feel.

So what do you do? Count to 10, sigh a few times and breathe deeply.
Calm down. Think. Find ways to get out of this conflict by:

* talking it over quietly, later on – example 1.
* getting out of a difficult situation, taking another route – example 2.
* adjusting to the situation: If you can't do it right, just do your best, not today but tomorrow – the last example.
* having someone else answer the question for you: calling for your big brother or sending your parents.

Having a good fight and making up afterwards is quite an art!

THE UNEXPECTED

Difficult moments have a tendency to spring up unexpectedly. You're unprepared, so they hit you harder. By training yourself, and working in this book, you'll be able to stand up to hard knocks much better. You know what might happen, why it happens and how to deal with it. The difficult moment isn't so unexpected, so it hits you less with less force!

Difficult moments are bound to come your way. And when they do, share them – at home, at school and with your friends. Sharing is healing.
It's especially good to write them down, to share them with your book. Every chapter has room for it, so don't hesitate to use it for this purpose.

Writing and reflecting help you cope, help you grow strong and sturdy. This is also called mental and emotional growth. You don't see it but you can feel it.

MY DIFFICULT MOMENT IN OTHERLAND

....

....

....

....

....

....

....

....

....

....

....

....

....

....

....

....

....

....

....

After writing all this down, you deserve a treat! How about a special exercise to relax.

A TREAT – A RELAXING EXERCISE

First take a comfortable seat.
Close your eyes and sigh a few times – nice and deep breaths.
Now open your eyes again and continue reading.
Imagine a delicious scoop of your favorite ice cream.
Put this big luscious scoop into a nice crispy cone or in between two waffles. Whatever you like best.
Now put another smaller scoop on top. Another one? Beautiful!
Now take another deep breath with your eyes closed. Can you see your delicious ice cream? Use your imagination. That's it - you've got it!

Open your eyes again and take another deep breath.

Now you take a little lick, and then another. Let it melt on your tongue.
Do you feel how cold and sweet it is, how soft and smooth in your mouth?
Swallow it.
Feel it sliding down your throat and landing in your stomach.
Feel the chill.
Now take another lick and then a mouthful.
Cold on your teeth, isn't it?
Now finish it – quick, before it melts. Mmmmmmmmmmmm
That was nice. And there was lots of it, too.

You deserved this treat. Now you're ready to move on to dealing with difficult moments.

People have come up with rules for this. They call them the 'win-win' rules. When everyone involved in a quarrel uses these rules, it helps end the quarrel. In this way everyone is a little right and a little wrong. No one loses face. And in the end everyone involved feels as if they've won. That's why they call them 'win-win' rules.

THE WIN-WIN RULES

It may seem strange at first, these win-win rules. But they work. When you're quarreling and fighting you don't want to stay angry that long. And the others usually feel the same. You both look for ways to make up, ways to solve the conflict.

The best way to do this is with the help of an impartial person, someone who can see the other side of the story. The different perspective! This could be a parent, a teacher or another adult. This person can then take the lead and act according to the win-win rules.

These are the rules:

1. Everyone takes time to cool off and calm down. Each person does this in his or her own way: sitting by yourself, taking a short run, taking time out or whatever works best.
2. Everyone takes a turn giving his or her opinion about the conflict using I-messages. No shouting, no name-calling, no blaming. I think, I feel, I am.
3. Next the other (or others) says how she thinks the first person sees the problem. This person repeats what the first person said by saying: so you think..., you feel..., you are...
4. Then both people take turns in explaining their roles in the conflict, again using I-messages: because I ... we had this conflict.
5. After seeing the different sides to the conflict there's now an opportunity to get together and come up with solutions.
6. Now shake hands with your 'sparring partner' or say something nice. No bad feelings. Be positive.

All the parties feel recognized. They both won because of the win-win rules.
This way there's a band-aid for everyone involved. It's like the time your mother gave your knee a kiss when you fell down. It didn't take away the pain, but it felt better.
In many difficult moments win-win rules will support you. Fortunately there are plenty of adults to help you this way.

To keep these rules in mind, here's a little rhyme.

Calm down, my friend
Be reasonable – and then
Just count to ten,
And begin again.

Stop and think.
Make the link:
Listen and learn.
Each takes a turn.

Then be wise
and compromise,
Say something nice.
And in the end
you should be friends.

This chapter 'Difficult moments' has now come to an end. It wasn't easy. In reality difficult moments aren't easy to handle, either. Don't forget to ask for help when you have difficulties.

Here's a short list of the contents to help you memorize now and browse later.

A SHORT LIST

In this chapter you learned that:

* relating to others in a new language easily leads to difficulties,
* these difficulties can be solved,
* you can learn how to do this with the help of new rules,
* there's a new rhyme to support you.

In the next chapter we'll talk about the feelings all people have who are living abroad for a longer period of time. That chapter will tell you about homesickness and how to deal with it.

Once again here's a page for your diary. This is where you can write down all the things you don't want to forget as well as your questions and comments. Add your pictures and drawings, too, just as you did in the other chapters.

MY DIARY

Chapter **9**

Homesick

In the previous chapters you created pieces in your book that fit into the secret of Otherland. You wrote, drew and reflected on life in another country and what it meant for you – how so much is different, and how different can be normal, too. You learned about going to school for the first time. All those new words! You set out and tried to make friends. If quarrels threatened to break out, you now know how to handle them. So the name of the last chapter was 'Difficult moments'.
But there may be more difficult moments to come, not in your relationships with others but with yourself. Maybe you've already felt them, times when you wanted to hide in a dark corner and dream of your native country, your friends and your family, way back home. That's called being homesick. This is what we'll talk about now.

EATING PANCAKES

The word 'homesick' says exactly what it means: you feel sick, sick from longing for your home. It's a feeling that can even be painful. Did you ever feel it?

So what does eating pancakes – the name of this section – have to do with being homesick?

Well, let me explain. What a treat it is when a steaming hot stack of delicious, freshly made pancakes is put on the table! First there's the wonderful smell of frying, and now you're eager to dig in. Here's the first couple of pancakes, covered in syrup or jam, still warm. Mmmmmmm. Of course you'll have some more! There are plenty. These are delicious, too. But thirds? Maybe not. Oh, come on – smothered in butter and syrup. And then?! All of a sudden you've had your fill. No more pancakes for you. You'd like a fresh drink. And tomorrow no more pancakes!

You can compare your life in Otherland to eating pancakes. Of course a comparison isn't totally complete, but still…
In the beginning life in Otherland was great. You left home well prepared, and hopefully you were looking forward to what might happen next. Then came moving, the great journey, pulling up your roots and spreading your wings like a bird. You experienced new and exciting adventures. There was never a dull day. You solved the difficult moments with the help of your parents or friends. Your book helps you, too. It's like eating your first stack of pancakes: delicious, beautiful.

During that time life in Otherland means finding a new rhythm. You're getting used to everything new. Of course you still like it, but now and then you become irritated by small things. You get tired of the ongoing struggle to master the language, find new friends or deal with other inconveniences like the weather, the dust, the traffic and the noise – things you can't change but must learn to live with. There are some disappointments. You yourself are well aware of what they are. Now you start comparing life in Otherland to life in your homeland. You compare more things, more often.

And once again, it's like eating pancakes. This time imagine eating seconds and thirds. And then, all of a sudden, one morning you wake up and you've had enough. Otherland is no good at all. You'd give anything to go back home. You're fed up. Does this sound familiar? Of course! This is your last stack of pancakes. You don't want any more. You're longing for your favorite candy, your old friends to chat with, and family and neighbors dropping by. You may think of more things you miss. You seem to forget the tedious things about your homeland, and you forget the nice things about Otherland, too. Memory makes the past more beautiful, and the present becomes uglier. You long desperately for days gone by: this is called being homesick. You could show in your book what it's like to feel homesick. Later on you might remember, because later you'll still be thinking that life in the past was more beautiful... Fortunately you'll forget that you were homesick as well.

I'M FEELING DOWN AND I MISS

....

....

....

....

....

....

....

....

....

....

....

....

....

....

....

....

....

....

....

You noticed how in the beginning life in Otherland was like eating pancakes. But that's the end of the comparison. Because you don't eat pancakes for breakfast every day. Tomorrow morning you'll eat something different, and the day after that you may eat something different, too. But life in Otherland keeps going on, day after day after day – even when you're fed up with it. How will you deal with this?

OUT OF THE DUMPS

It's up to you to find a way to get over your homesickness. No one can do that for you. Feeling unhappy is not nice at all, but you shouldn't stay down in the dumps for long. Try to shake this mood! You can do this in different ways. I'll show you how. You'll have to do it by yourself, though, and make yourself strong enough to overcome these feelings. It's a pity there's no aspirin to take away this kind of pain. But read on to learn about your self-help 'medicine'.

1. First, accept that you're homesick. Nothing wrong with that. Everyone living abroad has to deal with it now and then, sooner or later. You don't have the flu, you're not overtired, you're just moody, bored or feeling out of sync because you're homesick.

2. Now that you know what's going on, get up and get out. Set out to meet other people, other kids. Try to make contact – pick some flowers in your garden and take them to someone. Find some book about your homeland. Then show it to someone and tell stories about it. Organize some games or join in with others. Make up your mind to do something for or with another person. While you're doing this you won't have time to focus on yourself.

3. Make your own room or your own corner especially comfortable. Search for some nice pictures or beautiful drawings and pin them on the walls. Play your favorite music, a computer game or what else you prefer. Chatting on the internet, if you have the facilities, is a help, too.

4. In the meantime, take it easy. Don't do everything at the same time. Go to bed early! Hard? Yes, but it helps.

5. Schedule your day. Your parents will help you, if you ask them. Wake up at the same time, go to bed at the same time, have your meals at fixed times. Do this everyday. You're building a new rhythm for yourself. Your body likes it and so will you.

6. Cry, laugh, sing and shout. Just let your feelings out. Go with the flow. Draw, write and paint, as you do in this book. Dance to the music in your room – or out in the garden! It may sound crazy, but it works. It relaxes and improves your mood. Try it!

7. Keep up your sports. Go on with your hobbies. Keep learning Otherlandish and use the language, too.

8. Talk about your feelings, about being homesick, at home and with your friends. Together you might even be able to joke about it, too. 'Misery loves company'.

These are my suggestions for getting over sadness or bad moods. Try and see what works best for you. Maybe one thing will work one day and another thing another day! Maybe a telephone call to a friend you miss so badly is a good idea as well. Don't give up! Do something, act – and you'll watch your misery, confusion and dislike disappear. You have to work on yourself to strengthen your own will. You have to want to grow and learn from what you don't yet understand. Give yourself a pat on your back!
Then you won't turn into a scared mouse, just hiding in a hole, too afraid to go out and enjoy life! Or a hare, running for his life because he's afraid of the unknown…

All this good advice was passed on to me by students who are familiar with homesickness themselves – kids who tried to solve their problems their own way, kids who became stronger and sturdier as they went along. I'm sure it will work for you, too. And you'll find your own solutions that work even better for you! You can pass them on to others as well, since this advice also works in other difficult emotional situations. Now I'll give you some real life examples of children of the world, writing and talking about their feelings of homesickness.

EXAMPLES

'When I'm feeling homesick, I go and play merry songs on the piano.' Jolande in Zimbabwe.

'When I'm down I always go jogging, then I take a hot shower.' Michael in Ecuador
'My favorite CD and a beautiful book help me.' Jan in Canada.
'I prefer writing about the things that are happening to us.' Frits in New Zealand.
'I take photos of my family and make a game of cards.' Duifje in Holland.

PARTNER IN DISTRESS

Maybe you'll find a friend who knows what homesickness feels like, who knows about feeling down. Chatting about the homesickness questions below could be fun. Or try the internet. You could also talk about it with your family. You may find out that you're not the only one who misses your homeland. You can help each other, and that makes you feel better, too.

You know,
said the hare to the fox,
it's only now,
I begin to see
how nice life used to be....

By Jove!!
said the fox to the hare,
now that we're here
we're no longer there.
So let's enjoy, my friend,
the pleasures of this land!

Instead of chatting about the following questions with friends, partners in distress or family members, try to find answers on your own. Write them down in your book, and later on try answering them again. Then you'll see how your feelings and thoughts have changed!

HOMESICK QUESTIONS

* What do you miss most of all?
* when does it hit you hardest?
* always at the same time of day, like when it starts getting dark?
* when you listen to a certain type of music?
* when you smell a certain familiar scent?
* or more often when you're in bed just before falling asleep?
* did you have these feelings before? When staying with friends for a weekend?
* what works best for you to get over it?

MY ANSWERS TO THE HOMESICK QUESTIONS

The thing I miss most is

....

....

It hits me when

....

....

I (never) used to be homesick when I

....

....

What works best for me is to

....

....

You've come to the end of chapter 9. You've read about homesickness, about eating pancakes and being fed up. You can feel how you're growing and getting stronger, and you understand the importance of following a rhythm.

Here's a short list of the contents to help you memorize now and browse later.

A SHORT LIST

In this chapter you learned that:

* homesickness hits you all of a sudden,
* now you know how to recognize it,
* there are ways to overcome it,

* getting a grip on yourself and on your feelings is helpful,
* now you know how to do this,
* you should give yourself a treat every now and then by relaxing.

And to finish this chapter, have another nice ice cream! You deserve it.

Back home you thought,
how nice will it be,
this Otherland to see!

Now in Otherland you dream,
How I pine,
for this homeland of mine!

And yet you still manage!

In the next chapter we'll focus on new thoughts to develop if you're living in Otherland for a longer period of time. Now here's another page for your diary.

MY DIARY

Chapter 10

We and they

Now that we're near the end of your book, let's return to Friends, family and festivities, chapter 7, do you remember? With all your new knowledge, see how you would deal with the following event I once saw happening.

Imagine the playground or recreation area near your school. It's recess and all the kids are playing and amusing themselves. You're joining them and you get along well. You're playing a ball game with an Otherland friend. All of a sudden a group of tall boys shows up, takes away your ball. 'This ball is meant for Otherlanders,' they say in a mean, teasing way. They start playing football with it. This is something you never expected. What do you do now?

WHAT YOU KNOW

In the previous chapters you read quite a bit about situations like this. But you were never confronted with this kind of behavior. So you apply the system:

Stop and look,
listen and ask.

Stop and look,
listen and think;

There was more to know,
so have another go.

This is easier said than done in a situation like this. At any rate, you stop. Don't do anything. You might be so angry that you'd like a fight. Or maybe you're so afraid that you'd like to run. Both actions are not effective – you know that now. First calm down and try to find a solution with your friend. Doing nothing at all could be a solution. After calming down you might talk it over with a teacher. The teacher might also include the aggressive boys.

Try to figure out why you're so angry and hurt. In your home country you would have been angry, too, but now you're also angry because you, as a foreigner, can't play with the ball. Why not? You didn't expect this. *Ask, listen and learn…* Find a solution together. If you don't succeed ask for help.

QUESTION

What would you do in such a difficult situation on the playground?
Why would you do that?

MY ANSWER, MY REACTION

When small quarrels or misunderstandings grow into constant teasing and bullying with a particular purpose, something else is the matter. Kids use it to show that you don't belong to their group. This is called discrimination. This cannot be allowed, so parents will talk this over in school with the teachers and the head of the school. Sometimes other parents are involved as well. It is not up to you to solve this problem. To you it's a nuisance, but you usually cannot put an end to this on your own. Help is needed.

UNEXPECTED EVENTS

You've done your best reading and working in this book. As I promised in the beginning, it's sure to help you. Even so, it doesn't mean that life in Otherland will be easy and predictable. This book is not like cough medicine that will take away the cough. Amazing things will keep on happening. And you'll still have to deal with them. The unexpected reactions of the people around you will often be mysterious to you and your family.

The moment you start learning from these events, life will start being more interesting as well as just plain complicated. Then you'll see that you yourself can react in either an Otherland or a Homeland way. You're able to choose and to act accordingly.

EXAMPLES OF CHOICES IN BEHAVIOR

* If some kid asks you: 'Let's play together some time at my place', and this is something that people say in the US, you'll know it's mostly just a way of being nice to you. It's not a serious invitation. It's the American part of you that knows this, the homelander. You're with it.

If instead you expect a real invitation, a follow-up reaction, you'll be frustrated when nothing happens. You react in a homeland way. You're out of sync.
How you want to feel is something you have to choose for yourself.

* In Peru when you invite friends to arrive at a certain time, you may ask 'Will that be local time (which could easily be two hours later) or English time (no more than thirty minutes later)'. This way you won't get all excited when they show up two-and-a-half hours late for your party.

Again, this time you choose between the past and the present way of reacting.

* In the Philippines you play with the girls if you're an American girl. You act in the Philippine way. If you play there with American girls, the American boys may join in.

Here again you choose your own behavior.

It's good that you now know this is not a matter of good customs or bad customs. They're just different. When in Rome do as the Romans do. Now you know how it feels to change roles and become an Otherlander with American or British roots.

A POEM

Many, many years ago, Mr. Kipling, a poet who traveled widely, wrote the following poem about all this. In some ways the world looked different back then, but the way people thought about the world is something you'll recognize.

Father, Mother and Me,
Sister and Auntie say
All the people like us are We
And everyone else is They.
And They live over the sea
While we live over the way,
But – would you believe it?
– They look upon We
As only a sort of They!

We eat pork and beef
with cow-horn-handled knives.
They who gobble Their rice off a leaf
Are horrified out of Their lives.
While They who live up in a tree,
Feast on grubs and clay,
(Isn't it scandalous?) look upon We
as a simply disgusting They!

We eat kitcheny food.
We have doors that latch.
They drink milk and blood
under an open thatch.
We have doctors to fee.
They have wizards to pay.
(And impudent heathen!) They look upon We
as a quite impossible They!

All good people agree,
And all good people say,
All nice people, like us are We
and everyone else is They:
But if you cross over the sea,
instead of over the way,
You may end by (think of it!) looking on We
as only a sort of They!

R. Kipling, *We and They*

This is an old poem, but you see not much changed. It will be like this for you, too. You'll feel at home in Otherland after a while. How long? This depends on you, the country you go to and the country you come from. Anyway, you'll have learned more than any child who stays in her homeland, as this book now clearly shows.

RECYCLING THE BOOK

A wonderful thing is that you can sort of recycle this book. After a while, if something is troubling you or you're moving again, return to the book. Pick the relevant chapters or paragraphs and read them again. Buy a new notebook, put you name and date in it, and start a new diary. Use the same headings or do it in your new and better way. Then you can reflect on reality again and help yourself – just as you've been doing here.

By now you've nearly finished this book! In the next and final chapter you'll unlock the secret of Otherland.
First, here's a short list of the contents of chapter 10 to help you memorize now and browse later.

A SHORT LIST

In this chapter you read about:

* discrimination: how to recognize it and how to handle it,
* role changes; are you an American or British Otherlander or an Otherland-American or Otherland-Brit?
* how it's up to you to decide how to react,
* the new roots in Otherland and growing from 'They' into 'We'.

Of course there's still some room left for you to create your diary pages. Did you make any more beautiful paintings or pictures? Paste them in, too, and don't forget the photographs. Whenever you're back in your Homeland your family and friends will enjoy them. You'll be proud to show your own homemade book.

MY DIARY

Unlocking the secret

THE KEYS

Here we are, almost at the end of your book, and you're probably wondering, What is the secret of Otherland? At the beginning you may not have had any idea what the secret was. Go back to the beginning of the book and take a look. When you started you were completely at sea, just stumbling around. But the longer you read the more puzzle pieces you found with helpful advice. Life in Otherland started getting easier. Then a light must have gone on in your head. Those pieces have to fit in somewhere.

Take a minute to look for those pieces in each chapter. Draw them one by one in the big drawing, up in the clouds. You can color them in with the different colors from the chapters or fill them in with the key words. Copy the poems (or parts of them), or whatever you think is more important, in the sails or wherever you think they would look best. After all, this is your book, isn't it? The choice is up to you.

Now take a look! Use your imagination to show how your ship is going to sail through life in Otherland. You're in charge of the rudder, you're the skipper. You've got an entire crew on board. You've got Alice there to help you remember to ask a lot of questions and not start making judgments right away about all the things that are different.

Puss-in-Boots is coming with you to be your helper or to give you a hand in finding another friend. The fox has taught you how to make friends and how to be patient. And the hare reminds you that a good skipper can be afraid sometimes, too!

Don't forget your Otherland friends, on deck and below, and in the dinghy.
With a crew like that you'll go a long way.
As you sail your ship you'll have to keep a good eye on the wind and waves if you're to sail in safety. So *look and listen, listen and ask.* Look at the clouds, remember what's written there, and everything is sure to turn out all right.

The secret? You'll find that in the big drawing, which you can explain in your own way. Your whole book is there. You never would have understood any of this before, but now it's your secret.

SO NOW WHAT?

You might copy this drawing, maybe enlarge it and hang it in your own place so you won't easily forget your secret. Or you might keep this book and the drawing a secret, and put it in a secret place no one else knows about. Take it out if you want to read something from it again. But it's sure to be more fun if you share your secret with lots of other people!

Whenever you look at the drawing of the beautiful ship you're sailing on now you'll know just what to do to make things turn out all right, even when the waves are high.

I wish you a safe journey! Have lots of fun in Otherland!

1
2
3
4
5
6
7
8
9
10

Information

In this chapter you'll find more information on subjects you encountered in your book.

Addresses

Ministerie van Buitenlandse zaken, tel. Info: 070 3484770, www.bz.minbuza.nl
en www.stola/edu/network/travel-advisories.hhtml;

Stichting NOB, Parkweg 20 A, 2271 AJ Voorburg, tel. 070 3866646,
fax 070 3873154, E-mail stichting nob@snob.nl;

Radio Netherlands (Wereldomroep), P.O. Box 222, 1222 JG Hilversum,
tel.: +31 (0)35 672 43 33, wereldomroep@rnw.nl, www.wereldomroep.nl, www.rnw.nl

Radio Netherlands (Wereldomroep) is the Dutch international public broadcasting service. On radio, television and the Internet, Radio Netherlands provides news, information and culture in eight languages, reaching an average global audience of 50 million people. The sites www.wereldexpat.nl (adults) and www.wereldkids.nl (kids) are focussed on Dutch expatriates.

Intercultural Press, Yarmouth, Maine, USA, www.interculturalpress.com

Intercultural books for children

Alice in Wonderland, Caroll, Lewis, Penguin 2003

A life like mine. How children live around the world, Khan, J., Unicef (DK Publishing) 2002

Children just like me: Celebrations!, Kindersly, A., Kindersly, B., DK Publishing 1998

Children just like me, Kindersly, Anabel, Kindersly, B., Unicef (DK Publishing) 1995

Dangerous Skies, Fisher Staples, S., Farrar, Straus & Giroux 1996

Houses and homes (Around the world series), Morris, A., Shen's books 1995

How people live, Freeman, D., DK Publishing 2003

If the world were a village: a book about the world's people, Smith, David J., A&C Black 2004

Kids around the world celebrate! The best feasts and festivals from many lands, Jones, L., Wiley publishers 2000

Kids around the world cook! The best foods and recipes from many lands, Braman, A., Bosson, J., Wiley publishers 2000

The little prince, de Saint-Exupéry, A., Thorndike Press 2005

When Africa was home, Williams, K.L., New York 1991

www.crossculturalchildrenbooks.com

www.interculturalchildrenbooks.com

www.internationalchildrencookbooks.com

Reference material for educators, parents and other interested persons

Culture & Pedagogy, International comparisons in primary education, Alexander, R., Oxfort 2001

Emotional intelligence, Goleman, D., Bantam Dell 1997

Hidden immigrants: legacies of growing up abroad, Bell, L., Notre Dame 1997

Language and Culture in teaching and learning, Salo-Lee, L. & Winter-Tarvinen, A., Jyvaskyla 1995

Learning the skills of peacemaking, Drew, N., California 1987

Moving your family overseas, Kalb, R., Welch, P., Yarmouth, 1992

Notes from a traveling childwood, Cluskey, Mc, 1994

Romancing Vietnam, Wintle, J., Random House London 1992

The art of crossing cultures, Storti, C., Yarmouth, 1990

The expert expatriate, Hess, M.B., Linderman, P., Yarmouth, 2002

The nurture assumption / Why children turn out the way they do, Harris, J., Simon and Schuster 1998

The transcendent child: Tales of triumph over the past, Rubin, Lillian B., HarperCollins 1997

The whole world guide to culture learning, Hess, J. Daniel, Yarmouth 1994

Transcultural Odysseys, Shames, G., Yarmouth 1997

www.interculturalpress.com

www.kitpublishers.nl

THE FIRST EASY OTHERLANDISH WORDS I LEARNED

I am ....

I live ....

Will you please help me? ....

Good morning..

Hello ....

Bye ....

See you ....

Thank you..

What's your name?..

My name is ....

Where is? ....

Being able to count comes in handy too!

Look for help in finding the right answers, the correct pronunciation and then learn them by heart.